About the author and how to

Anthony Simpson is an author, speake. and survivors of human trafficking. He is deeply committed to building a bridge between victims and survivors and those who want to help them. With a background in social work and a deep understanding of the issues surrounding human trafficking, Anthony has dedicated his career to raising awareness and providing support to those affected by this devastating crime. He is a passionate and dedicated individual who is committed to making a difference in the lives of those who have been affected by human trafficking. Through his work as an author, speaker, and advocate, Anthony is helping to bring about change and provide hope for victims and survivors of this terrible crime.

If you would like to contact Anthony Simpson, you can connect with him on Instagram at @hardtoharm and on Twitter at @hardtoharm.

He is always happy to hear from people who are interested in learning more about human trafficking, how to help victims and survivors, or who would like to get involved in his advocacy work.

Anthony Simpson also has a community group called "Hard To Harm" which aims to bring awareness and provide support to victims and survivors of human trafficking. Anyone who is interested in joining this community can do so through the Telegram link https://t.me/+Kp5EJ1MhBgw5ZjVh or through the links in the description of the social media pages previously mentioned (Instagram and Twitter).

The Hard To Harm community is a supportive and empowering space where individuals can connect with others who are working towards a common goal of ending human trafficking and helping victims and survivors. Joining this group will give you the opportunity to learn from Anthony and other advocates, stay informed about the latest developments in the fight against human trafficking, and participate in various events and initiatives.

Important Note For The Reader:

The author generated this text in part with GPT-3, OpenAI's large-scale language-generation model. Upon generating draft language, the author reviewed, edited, and revised the language to their own liking and takes ultimate responsibility for the content of this publication.

Table of Contents

Introduction
The purpose 9
The layout of this book 10

1. **Chapter 1: How to understand and address human trafficking**

Introduction 12
Do's and Don'ts 13
Importance of volunteering or finding a mentor 14
How to get connected without being rejected 15
Why you should not do this alone 16
How to find like minded people to partner with 18

2. **Chapter 2: How to rescue victims of human trafficking**

Introduction 20
Is rescuing victims anything like the movies 20
How rescue can be done very wrong 21
Rescue is still a worthy endeavor 23
15 career opportunities 24
More about these careers 26
Knowing multiple languages can be very useful 28
Which languages are available to learn 29
Want to kick down doors? These are the careers for you 30
Average salaries for these careers 31

3. **Chapter 3: How to educate and prevent human trafficking: Careers, entrepreneurship, and community action**

Introduction 33
Why education/prevention is important 33
The value of raising awareness 34
20 education and prevention careers 35
Education and prevention pros and cons 37
No college degree? No problem, here's what you can do! 38
10 certification programs 39
Want to start your own education/prevention business? 40
How to monetize your business 41
Do's and don'ts for starting and education/prevention business 43
Starting college clubs and nonprofits 45
The impact of starting a college campus club for education/prevention 46
College club success stories 47
Easier ways to start a club 48
Ways to create an education/prevention club 49
Discussion questions for your new campus club 51
All about non-profits 52
Have a very specific vision for your non-profit 53
How to start a non-profit 54
10 ways your non-profit could fail 55
Non-profit do's and don'ts 56
Further research suggestions 58
Conclusion 60

4. **Chapter 4: How to restore and rehabilitate survivors of human trafficking**

Introduction 62
Restoration and rehabilitation 63
Importance of a trauma informed approach 63
What careers can you get into? 64
20 careers for you 65
Pros and cons of careers in restoration and rehabilitation 68

Education outside of colleges and universities 70
15 online resources for training programs 72
Business ideas for entrepreneurs 74
20 ideas for a new business 75
Do's and don'ts for starting a restoration / rehabilitation business 78
College clubs and non profits 79
The impact you can have if you start one 80
8 Examples that have made a real impact 81
How to make starting a club more efficient 83
How to create a restoration/rehabilitation club 84
Discussion questions for your new club 86
Resources for starting a non-profit 87
Be very specific when starting an organization 88
A guide for non-profits 89
Recommended books starting a non-profit 90
Why non-profits fail and yours will not 91
Non-profit do's and don'ts 92
Resources to look into 94
Conclusion 95

5. **Chapter 5: How to combat human trafficking: Strategies for legislation and activism**

Introduction 97
Current state of legislation and activism 97
The importance of human trafficking legislation and prevention 98
Understanding current legislation 99
10 key federal and state laws 101
15 anti-trafficking laws passed by cities 103
How these laws are enforced and their limitations 105
International human trafficking laws and treaties 106
Want to learn more on international policy? 107
Advocacy and activism 108
What laws can you advocate for local change? 109
Raising awareness for your community 111
15 examples of grassroots movements 112
Grassroots organizations 116

How individuals and organizations can make a difference 116
The best ways to build partnerships 118
How can technology be used to support grassroots organizing efforts? 120
Working with government and policy makers 121
How individuals and organizations can organize effectively 121
Media and communication strategies 123
Examples of partnerships with governments and policy makers 124
Conclusion 126

Bonus: 79 anti-trafficking careers, jobs and business opportunities for the modern day abolitionist

1. Case Manager
2. Community outreach worker
3. Data analyst
4. Educator
5. Forensic interviewer
6. Government relations specialist
7. Human rights lawyer
8. Human trafficking investigator
9. Immigration lawyer
10. Intelligence analyst
11. Law enforcement Analyst
12. Law enforcement Officer
13. Medical professional
14. Mental health counselor
15. Non-profit manager
16. Public health professional
17. Public policy advocate
18. Program Evaluator
19. Researcher
20. Social worker
21. Survivor Advocate
22. Trafficking-specific support group facilitator
23. Trainer
24. Victim advocate
25. Airline employee

26. Business consultant
27. Business owner
28. Employee benefits specialist
29. Entrepreneur
30. Financial analyst
31. Fundraiser
32. Grant writer
33. Grocery store owner
34. Human resources professional
35. Investor
36. Philanthropist
37. Port worker
38. Recruiter
39. Specialty food store owner
40. Supply chain professional
41. Talent acquisition specialist
42. Activist
43. Community leader
44. Event planner
45. Filmmaker
46. Fundraiser
47. Graphic designer
48. Journalist
49. Lobbyist
50. Media specialist
51. Philanthropy professional
52. Photographer
53. Pollster
54. Political campaign worker
55. Public official
56. Public opinion researcher
57. Public speaker
58. Religious leader
59. Social media manager
60. Anthropologist
61. Economist
62. Historian

63. Journalist
64. Government relations specialist
65. Sociologist
66. Artificial intelligence specialist
67. Blockchain specialist
68. Civil affairs officer
69. Cyber warfare officer
70. Legal officer
71. Logistics officer
72. Military intelligence officer
73. Cybercrime investigator
74. Digital forensics analyst
75. Intelligence analyst
76. Open source intelligence analyst
77. Social media intelligence analyst
78. Threat intelligence analyst
79. Web intelligence analyst

Introduction

"How to Fight Human Trafficking Today: A comprehensive How-To Guide For Anyone Who Wants to Make a Difference"

Dear friend,

We stand together in our shared passion to fight human trafficking, a heinous crime that robs countless individuals of their freedom and dignity. You are not alone in feeling overwhelmed and unsure of how to make a meaningful impact in this battle. But know that every small action, no matter how insignificant it may seem, can bring us closer to a world where trafficking no longer exists.

With this book, we hope to empower you with the knowledge and tools needed to take meaningful action and make a real difference in the fight against human trafficking. Together, we can work towards a brighter future for all.

-Anthony Simpson

The Purpose

This book serves not only as a guide to the various ways in which you can take action against human trafficking but also as a support system as you navigate the complexities of dedicating your life to this cause. We understand that the fight against human trafficking can feel overwhelming and that it is important to have a comprehensive understanding of the many ways in which you can make a difference.

Our goal is to provide you with a comprehensive, yet not exhaustive, breakdown of the different methods and strategies for ending human trafficking. We will explore both traditional and innovative approaches and provide you with the necessary resources and information to make informed decisions about how you want to dedicate your time, energy and resources to this important cause.

We believe that through understanding, compassion and collective action, we can work towards a world where human trafficking is a thing of the past. Let us support you in your journey of dedicating your life to this cause."

The Layout of This Book

This book is divided into five sections, each focusing on a specific aspect of the fight against human trafficking. In the first section, we will explore the complexities of human trafficking, including understanding the root causes and the different forms it takes. This will give you a comprehensive understanding of the issue, which will be vital in making informed decisions about how you want to take action.

The second section is dedicated to understanding the rescue process for victims of human trafficking. This includes understanding the signs of trafficking, ways to report it, and the different organizations and groups that work towards rescuing victims.

The third section of the book focuses on the importance of education and prevention in ending human trafficking. This includes understanding how to identify and prevent trafficking and ways in which individuals and communities can work together to create a safer environment.

The fourth section focuses on the rehabilitation and restoration process for survivors of human trafficking. This includes understanding the long-term effects of trafficking on individuals, the different types of support and services available and how to best support survivors in their healing journey.

The fifth section focuses on the importance of legislation and activism in ending human trafficking. This includes understanding the laws and policies related to human trafficking, ways in which individuals can advocate for change and ways to support organizations that work towards passing legislation to combat trafficking.

One of the most powerful tools in the fight against human trafficking is the ability to come together with others who share the same passion and purpose. As Frederick Douglass, a famous abolitionist, said, "If there is no struggle, there is no progress." These discussion questions are intended to spark meaningful conversations, foster collaboration and inspire individuals to take action.

It is important to note that all four methods can happen simultaneously. However, we recommend starting with one method and going deep into it before moving on to another. It is better to go a mile deep and an inch wide rather than an inch deep and a mile wide. Like planting a seed, you want to focus on one area to make it grow strong before moving on to another, rather than spreading out your resources and not seeing the full potential of any one method.

Throughout the book, we will provide you with the resources and information necessary to make informed decisions about how you want to dedicate your time, energy, and resources to this important cause. We believe that through understanding, compassion, and collective action, we can work towards a world where human trafficking is a thing of the past.

Chapter 1: How to Understand and Address Human Trafficking

Introduction

The fight against human trafficking is one of the most important and pressing issues of our time. It is a crime that affects millions of people around the world, often leading to devastating consequences for those who are caught in its web. Unfortunately, despite the best intentions of many, the fight against human trafficking is often hindered by a lack of understanding and knowledge about the issue.

One example of this is when well-intentioned individuals or organizations attempt to rescue victims of trafficking without fully understanding the complexities of the situation. This can lead to poorly planned and executed rescue operations that put victims at further risk. In some cases, these efforts have even resulted in the re-trafficking of victims or the separation of families.

Another example is when individuals or organizations use sensationalized or inaccurate information to raise awareness about human trafficking. This can lead to a distorted understanding of the issue and can also harm victims by stigmatizing them or undermining their efforts to rebuild their lives.

It is crucial that we handle this issue with care and sensitivity, and that we approach it with a deep understanding of the complexities and nuances of human trafficking. We must recognize that there are no easy solutions to this problem and that meaningful progress can only be made through a collaborative and evidence-based approach.

As we begin this journey of understanding and fighting human trafficking, it is important to remember that our actions have real-life consequences for real people. Let us not be guilty of doing more harm than good. Let us educate ourselves, and act with compassion and purpose.

Do's and Don'ts

Do's:

1. Educate yourself about the issue of human trafficking. This includes understanding the different forms of trafficking, such as sex trafficking and labor trafficking, as well as the root causes and contributing factors. Resources for further education include the UN Office on Drugs and Crime (UNODC) and the Polaris Project.
2. Support organizations that work directly with victims of human trafficking. Look for organizations that have a strong track record of providing comprehensive services, such as legal assistance, counseling, and housing. Organizations such as the International Justice Mission and A21 are good places to start.
3. Be aware of the signs of human trafficking. This includes recognizing the indicators of physical abuse, such as bruises or burns, as well as more subtle signs such as signs of control or manipulation.
4. Support policies and legislation that addresses human trafficking. This includes supporting laws that increase penalties for traffickers and provide support and services for victims.
5. Be a responsible consumer. Be aware of the products and services you purchase and how they may be connected to human trafficking.

Don'ts:

1. Do not assume that all individuals involved in the commercial sex industry are victims of trafficking. Many people choose to

enter this field and should not be stigmatized or criminalized for it.
2. Do not participate in "rescue" operations without proper training and understanding of the complexities of human trafficking. These efforts can put victims at further risk and can also lead to the separation of families.
3. Do not use sensationalized or inaccurate information to raise awareness about human trafficking. This can lead to a distorted understanding of the issue and can also harm victims by stigmatizing them or undermining their efforts to rebuild their lives.
4. Do not blame or stigmatize victims of human trafficking. They are not responsible for their exploitation and need support and understanding.
5. Do not generalize the issue of human trafficking. It is a complex issue that affects many different communities and individuals and can take many different forms.
6. Do not rely on stereotypes and myths when identifying human trafficking victims. These can lead to misidentification and can also harm innocent people.

It is important to note that human trafficking is a complex issue that requires a comprehensive approach. It is important to educate ourselves, support organizations and policies that address the issue, and act in ways that are sensitive and compassionate toward the victims. It is also important to continue learning and stay informed about the latest research and best practices in the fight against human trafficking.

Importance of Volunteering or Finding a Mentor

Volunteering with a reputable organization or learning from a local or online mentor can be an amazing way to gain valuable knowledge and experience in the fight against human trafficking.

Working with a reputable organization allows individuals to learn from experienced professionals who have dedicated their careers to this cause. They can provide guidance and advice on how to effectively address the issue, as well as share valuable insights and lessons learned from their own experiences. This can help individuals to avoid common mistakes and to develop more effective strategies for addressing human trafficking.

Mentors, whether local or online, can also provide valuable guidance and support. They can share their own experiences and offer advice on how to navigate the complexities of the issue. This can be especially valuable for individuals who are just starting out in the fight against human trafficking, as mentors can provide a sounding board for ideas and help to guide decision-making.

Both volunteering and mentorship provide individuals with the opportunity to see the issue from different perspectives, learn from real-life examples, and gain a deeper understanding of the complexities of human trafficking. They can also help individuals to develop a network of contacts and resources that can be valuable as they continue to work on this issue.

It is important to note that when looking for a reputable organization or mentor it is essential to conduct research, read reviews and testimonials, and ask for referrals from trusted sources. This will ensure that the organization or mentor is reliable and that the individual's time and energy will be well spent.

Overall, volunteering with a reputable organization or learning from a local or online mentor can be an amazing way to gain valuable knowledge and experience in the fight against human trafficking. These opportunities can help individuals to avoid common mistakes, develop more effective strategies, and make a meaningful impact in the fight against this crime.

How to Get Connected Without Being Rejected

Connecting with reputable organizations or mentors in the fight against human trafficking can be a valuable way to gain knowledge and experience, but it can also be challenging to get accepted and not be rejected.

An evidence-based approach can increase the chances of being accepted by these organizations or mentors. This approach includes researching the organization or mentor, looking at their track record, and understanding their mission and goals. It also includes understanding what they are looking for in a volunteer or mentee and how they evaluate potential candidates.

Networking is also important when connecting with organizations or mentors. As the best-selling networking book, "Never Eat Alone" by Keith Ferrazzi states, "Networking is not about hunting for jobs, it's about hunting for relationships." Building relationships with organizations or mentors takes time and effort, but it can lead to valuable connections and opportunities.

Another best-selling networking book, "The Art of Connecting: How to Overcome Differences, Build Rapport, and Communicate Effectively with Anyone" by Michael J. Gelb, suggests that one of the best ways to connect with others is by being genuinely interested in them. This means taking the time to understand their interests and goals, and being willing to offer support and assistance.

In addition, it is important to be persistent but not pushy. Organizations and mentors receive many requests for help and support, and it is essential to respect their time and decision-making process. As the book "The Power of Persistence" by Brian Tracy states, "The greatest difference between successful people and unsuccessful people is persistence."

Finally, it is important to be flexible and open to different opportunities. As the book "The Art of Possibility" by Rosamund Stone Zander and Benjamin Zander states, "The most powerful thing you can do to change the world is to change the way you see the world." Being open to different opportunities and perspectives can lead to unexpected connections and growth.

Connecting with reputable organizations or mentors in the fight against human trafficking can be challenging, but it is possible. An evidence-based approach, networking, being genuinely interested, persistent but not pushy, and being open to different opportunities can increase the chances of being accepted and making valuable connections.

Why You Should Not Do This Alone

The fight against human trafficking can be a daunting and overwhelming task, and it can be tempting to try to tackle it alone. However, as the saying goes, "if you want to go fast, go alone. If you want to go far, go together."

Working alone can lead to a sense of isolation and burnout. It can also limit your resources and networks, as well as the impact you can make. As the book "The Power of Intentional Leadership" by John C. Maxwell states, "Leadership is not about being in charge. It's about taking care of those in your charge." Working alone can be detrimental to your well-being and the people you want to help.

Collaboration and partnerships are key to making a meaningful impact in the fight against human trafficking. As the book "The Power of Collaboration: How to Create a Winning Team in Business and in Life" by Michael K. Simpson states, "Collaboration is the key to unlocking the full potential of any team, organization, or community." By working with others, you can share resources, knowledge, and ideas, and you can also multiply your efforts and reach more people.

Working with others can also provide a sense of community and support. As the book "The Five People You Meet in Heaven" by Mitch Albom states, "Each affects the other, and the other affects the next, and the world is full of stories, but the stories are all one." Working together can provide a sense of belonging and shared purpose, which can be especially important in a fight as challenging as human trafficking.

It is important to remember that you are not alone in this fight. There are many organizations, individuals, and groups working towards the same goal, and by joining forces, you can make a greater impact. As the book "The 7 Habits of Highly Effective People" by Stephen Covey states, "Strength lies in differences, not in similarities." Working together with different perspectives, skills, and resources can lead to more comprehensive and effective solutions.

The fight against human trafficking is not one that should be tackled alone. Collaboration and partnerships are key to making a meaningful impact, and working with others can provide support, resources, and a sense of community. It is important to remember that there are many organizations, individuals, and groups working towards the same goal and by joining forces, you can go much further than you could alone.

How to Find Like-Minded People to Partner With

There are a variety of ways to find like-minded individuals and organizations who share your passion for fighting human trafficking. One of the most effective ways is through online platforms.

Social media platforms such as Facebook, Twitter, and Instagram are excellent places to start. Many organizations and individuals working to combat human trafficking have active accounts on these platforms and use them to share information, resources, and updates on their efforts. By following these accounts, you can stay informed about the latest developments in the fight against human trafficking and connect with others who share your passion.

Another effective online platform is online forums and discussion boards. Websites such as Reddit and Quora have active communities discussing various topics related to human trafficking. By participating in these forums and discussions, you can connect with others who share your interests and learn from their experiences.

LinkedIn is also a great platform for professional networking, connecting with organizations and individuals working in the field of human trafficking, and finding a relevant job or volunteer opportunities.

Lastly, joining online groups and communities dedicated to the fight against human trafficking can also be a valuable way to connect with like-minded individuals. Websites such as Meetup and Eventbrite have a variety of groups and events related to human trafficking, where you can connect with others who share your passion and learn more about the issue.

It is also important to note that it is crucial to verify the authenticity of any online platforms, groups, or communities before getting involved, as there are many fake or misleading sources that can lead to misinformation or harm. It is always best to do your research, read reviews and testimonials, and ask for referrals from trusted sources.

There are a variety of online platforms available to connect with like-minded individuals and organizations working to combat human trafficking. Social media platforms, online forums and discussion boards, LinkedIn, and online groups and communities are all excellent places to start. By participating in these online communities, you can stay informed about the latest developments in the fight against human trafficking and connect with others who share your passion.

Chapter 2: How to Rescue Victims of Human Trafficking

Introduction

The movie 'Taken' portrays human trafficking as a sinister, far-off problem, one that only happens to other people in other countries. In reality, human trafficking is a pervasive and insidious issue that affects people from all walks of life, all over the world. It is not just a problem for law enforcement and government officials, but for all of us. In this chapter, we will explore the reality of human trafficking, and the ways in which we can all take action to rescue its victims. We will also examine how popular perceptions of human trafficking, like those portrayed in 'Taken', can actually make the problem worse by perpetuating harmful stereotypes and overlooking the complex, nuanced realities of the issue.

Is Rescuing Victims Anything Like the Movie *Taken*?

Rescuing victims of human trafficking is a complex and challenging task that requires a multi-disciplinary approach. According to the United Nations Office on Drugs and Crime (UNODC), rescuing victims of human trafficking involves providing them with immediate assistance, protection and support, as well as ensuring that they are not re-trafficked or penalized for crimes committed as a result of their trafficking experience.

The process of rescuing victims of human trafficking typically involves the following steps: identification, referral, protection, and reintegration. Identification refers to the process of identifying and locating victims of trafficking, which can be done through various means such as law enforcement operations, outreach efforts, or tips from the community. Referral refers to the process of connecting victims with appropriate services and support, such as emergency shelter, medical and mental health care, legal assistance, and social services. Protection refers to the provision of safe and secure housing, as well as legal and other forms of protection, to ensure that victims are not re-trafficked or harmed. Reintegration refers to the process of helping victims to return to their families, communities, or countries of origin and to rebuild their lives.

Rescuing victims of human trafficking requires a collaborative effort between various actors, including law enforcement, non-governmental organizations, and government agencies. According to a report by the International Labour Organization (ILO), law enforcement plays a crucial role in rescuing victims by identifying and arresting traffickers, as well as protecting and assisting victims. NGOs also play an important role in rescuing victims by providing critical services such as shelter, medical and mental health care, legal assistance, and social services. Government agencies, such as immigration authorities and social services departments, also have a critical role to play in rescuing victims by providing legal and other forms of protection, as well as assistance with reintegration.

It is important to note that there are also a lot of organizations and people who are not qualified and capable of rescuing victims from human trafficking, as the task is complex and requires specialized knowledge, skills, and resources. It is crucial that the task is done by qualified and trained professionals to ensure that the victims receive the best possible support and protection.

References:
- UNODC (United Nations Office on Drugs and Crime). (2020). Global Report on Trafficking in Persons. UNODC.
- ILO (International Labour Organization). (2018). Combating forced labor: A handbook for employers and business. ILO.
- Polaris. (2021). Identifying and responding to human trafficking. Polaris.

Rescue Can Be Done Very Wrong

Individuals and organizations who are not properly trained or qualified to rescue victims of human trafficking can cause far more harm than good. For example, well-intentioned but untrained individuals may inadvertently put victims at risk by not properly identifying them or by mishandling sensitive information. Similarly, organizations that are not well-versed in the complexities of human trafficking may not be equipped to provide appropriate support and protection to victims.

One example of this is the case of "rescue industry" in the Philippines, a phenomenon that emerged in the early 2000s, where foreign organizations and individuals, some of them Christian groups, would go to the Philippines to "rescue" alleged victims of sex trafficking. However, according to research by Rhacel Parreñas, these actions caused more harm than good. Many of the individuals who were deemed victims by these groups were in fact not trafficked, but voluntarily working in the sex industry. These "rescues" were often conducted without proper coordination with local authorities and without regard to the rights and autonomy of the individuals involved. This caused many individuals to be removed from their jobs, homes and support networks, and pushed them into more precarious and dangerous situations.

Another example is from the book "The Road of Lost Innocence" by Somaly Mam, a memoir about the author's experiences as a survivor of sex trafficking in Cambodia. The book describes how Mam, as the head of an anti-trafficking organization, helped to rescue and rehabilitate young girls who were victims of sex trafficking. However, it was later revealed that some of the stories in the book were fabricated and that Somaly Mam had lied about her past. This caused significant harm to the reputation of the organization and the anti-trafficking movement as a whole.

In both examples, the actions of these individuals and organizations were driven by a desire to help, but their lack of proper training and understanding of the issue led to unintended consequences that harmed the very people they were trying to help. It is crucial that individuals and organizations working to rescue victims of human trafficking are properly trained, qualified and work closely with other experts in the field to ensure they are making a positive impact.

References:
- Parreñas, R. (2011). Illicit Flirtations: Labor, Migration, and Sex Trafficking in Tokyo. Stanford University Press.
- Mam, S. (2009). The Road of Lost Innocence: The True Story of a Cambodian Heroine. Spiegel & Grau.

Rescue Is Still a Worthy Endeavor

Just because some individuals and organizations have caused harm in the past while trying to rescue victims of human trafficking, it does not mean that individuals and organizations cannot be a part of a system that does it right. In fact, it is crucial that individuals and organizations work together to fight human trafficking in a responsible and effective manner.

One way to ensure that individuals and organizations are doing the right thing is by working with established, reputable organizations that have a proven track record of successfully rescuing and supporting victims of human trafficking. These organizations typically have a deep understanding of the issue, as well as the necessary skills, resources, and relationships to effectively identify and assist victims. They also often have established partnerships with other organizations and government agencies that are essential in the fight against human trafficking.

Another way to ensure that individuals and organizations are doing the right thing is by participating in training and education programs that provide a comprehensive understanding of human trafficking. This includes understanding the different forms of trafficking, the dynamics of exploitation, the needs of victims, and the most effective ways of providing assistance and protection. By participating in such programs, individuals and organizations can develop the knowledge and skills necessary to effectively combat human trafficking.

Finally, it's important to keep in mind that rescuing victims of human trafficking is a continuous and long-term process that requires the participation and support of not only the government, non-profit organizations and law enforcement but also the general public. By raising awareness of the issue, supporting and volunteering with reputable organizations, and participating in advocacy efforts to bring an end to human trafficking, individuals and organizations can play an important role in the fight against human trafficking and make a positive impact in the lives of victims.

While it is true that some individuals and organizations have caused harm in the past while trying to rescue victims of human trafficking, it does not mean that it cannot be done right. By participating in reputable organizations, training and education programs and raising awareness, individuals and organizations can play a crucial role in fighting human trafficking and make a positive impact in the lives of victims.

15 Career Opportunities

One of the most important ways to combat human trafficking is through the work of dedicated professionals in a variety of fields. In this chapter, we will explore 15 career opportunities that can make a real impact in the fight against human trafficking. These include roles in law enforcement, social work, human rights law, immigration law, victim advocacy, NGO work, medicine, rehabilitation, translation, research, public policy, journalism, data analysis, fundraising and education. Each of these careers plays a critical role in rescuing victims, holding traffickers accountable, and ultimately ending human trafficking.

1. Law enforcement officer: Law enforcement officers play a crucial role in rescuing victims of human trafficking by identifying and arresting traffickers, as well as protecting and assisting victims.
2. Social worker: Social workers help victims of human trafficking by providing critical services such as counseling, case management, and support with finding housing and medical care.
3. Human rights lawyer: Human rights lawyers work to protect the rights of victims of human trafficking and hold traffickers accountable for their crimes.

4. Immigration Attorney: Immigration attorneys assist victims of human trafficking in obtaining legal status and protection in the country where they are seeking refuge.
5. Victim advocate: Victim advocates provide emotional support and advocacy for victims of human trafficking, connecting them with services and resources.
6. NGO staff member: NGO staffs help to rescue victims of human trafficking by providing critical services such as shelter, medical and mental health care, legal assistance, and social services.
7. Medical professional: Medical professionals provide medical care and support for victims of human trafficking, including trauma-informed care and mental health services.
8. Rehabilitation specialist: Rehabilitation specialists work with victims of human trafficking to help them recover from their experiences and reintegrate into society.
9. Translator/interpreter: Translators and interpreters play a critical role in rescuing victims of human trafficking by helping them communicate with law enforcement, medical professionals, and other service providers.
10. Researcher: Researchers study the causes and consequences of human trafficking and use their findings to inform policies and programs to combat the problem.
11. Public policy advocate: Public policy advocates work to influence laws and policies to better protect victims of human trafficking and hold traffickers accountable.
12. Journalist: Journalists raise awareness about human trafficking by reporting on the issue and shedding light on the experiences of victims.
13. Data analyst: Data analysts analyze data on human trafficking to identify patterns, trends and opportunities to intervene.
14. Fundraiser: Fundraisers help to support organizations and programs that rescue victims of human trafficking by raising money from donors.
15. Educator: Educators raise awareness about human trafficking and provide education on how to recognize and respond to the issue to a wide range of audiences.

It's important to note that these are not the only career opportunities to rescue victims of human trafficking and that many other careers can also play an important role in fighting human trafficking. Additionally, many of these careers require specific education and training, and it's important to research and plan accordingly before committing to a career path.

More About These Careers

1. Law enforcement officer: Law enforcement officers play a crucial role in rescuing victims of human trafficking by identifying and arresting traffickers, as well as protecting and assisting victims. According to the Bureau of Labor Statistics, the median annual salary for police and detectives is $64,490, and employment is projected to grow 4% from 2020 to 2030.
2. Social worker: Social workers help victims of human trafficking by providing critical services such as counseling, case management, and support with finding housing and medical care. According to the Bureau of Labor Statistics, the median annual salary for social workers is $61,230, and employment is projected to grow 11% from 2020 to 2030.
3. Human rights lawyer: Human rights lawyers work to protect the rights of victims of human trafficking and hold traffickers accountable for their crimes. According to the Bureau of Labor Statistics, the median annual salary for lawyers is $122,960, and employment is projected to grow 4% from 2020 to 2030.
4. Immigration Attorney: Immigration attorneys assist victims of human trafficking in obtaining legal status and protection in the country where they are seeking refuge. According to the Bureau of Labor Statistics, the median annual salary for lawyers is $122,960, and employment is projected to grow 4% from 2020 to 2030.
5. Victim advocate: Victim advocates provide emotional support and advocacy for victims of human trafficking, connecting them with services and resources. According to the Bureau of Labor Statistics, the median annual salary for social and

human service assistants is $35,460, and employment is projected to grow 11% from 2020 to 2030.
6. NGO staff member: NGO staff help to rescue victims of human trafficking by providing critical services such as shelter, medical and mental health care, legal assistance, and social services. The salary for NGO staff can vary widely depending on the specific organization and role, but according to Payscale, the average salary for a non-profit program manager is $54,000.
7. Medical professional: Medical professionals provide medical care and support for victims of human trafficking, including trauma-informed care and mental health services. According to the Bureau of Labor Statistics, the median annual salary for physicians and surgeons is $208,000, and employment is projected to grow 7% from 2020 to 2030.
8. Rehabilitation specialist: Rehabilitation specialists work with victims of human trafficking to help them recover from their experiences and reintegrate into society. According to the Bureau of Labor Statistics, the median annual salary for rehabilitation counselors is $35,950, and employment is projected to grow 9% from 2020 to 2030.
9. Translator/interpreter: Translators and interpreters play a critical role in rescuing victims of human trafficking by helping them communicate with law enforcement, medical professionals, and other service providers. According to the Bureau of Labor Statistics, the median annual salary for interpreters and translators is $52,830, and employment is projected to grow 19% from 2020 to 2030.
10. Researcher: Researchers study the causes and consequences of human trafficking and use their findings to inform policies and programs to combat the problem. According to Payscale, the average salary for a research analyst is $57,000.
11. Public policy advocate: Public policy advocates work to influence laws and policies to better protect victims of human trafficking and hold traffickers accountable. According to Payscale, the average salary for a policy analyst is $68,000.

12. Journalist: Journalists raise awareness about human trafficking by reporting on the issue and shedding light on the experiences of victims. According to the Bureau of Labor Statistics, the median annual salary for reporters and correspondents is $43,490, and employment is projected to decline 9% from 2020 to 2030.

13. Data analyst: Data analysts analyze data on human trafficking to identify patterns, trends, and opportunities to intervene. According to Payscale, the average salary for a data analyst is $65,000.
14. Fundraiser: Fundraisers help to support organizations and programs that rescue victims of human trafficking by raising money from donors. According to Payscale, the average salary for a fundraiser is $46,000.
15. Educator: Educators raise awareness about human trafficking and provide education on how to recognize and respond to the issue to a wide range of audiences. According to the Bureau of Labor Statistics, the median annual salary for postsecondary teachers is $79,540, and employment is projected to grow 4% from 2020 to 2030.

It's important to note that these salaries and job growth projections are estimates, and can vary depending on factors such as location, experience, and specific role. Additionally, many of these careers require specific education and training, and it's important to research and plan accordingly before committing to a career path.

Knowing Multiple Languages Can Be Very Useful

Being fluent in multiple languages can be a valuable asset for those who are interested in fighting human trafficking. This is because trafficking victims often come from diverse backgrounds and may speak languages other than English. Being able to communicate with them in their native language can help to build trust and facilitate the provision of services and support.

For example, if you're interested in working with victims of human trafficking in a legal setting, being able to speak the language of the victims can make it easier to obtain statements and evidence and to understand the context of the trafficking situation. Similarly, if you're interested in working in an NGO that provides services to victims, being able to speak their language can help to create a more welcoming and supportive environment.

Many organizations that work to combat human trafficking also have a global reach, and being able to speak multiple languages can open up opportunities for international travel and work. This can include working with international organizations, traveling to other countries to help rescue victims, and participating in international anti-trafficking initiatives.

There are also many resources available for learning new languages, both online and offline. Some options include taking classes at a local college or university, using online language-learning platforms such as Duolingo, Babbel, and Rosetta Stone, or hiring a private tutor. Additionally, some organizations that work on human trafficking also offer language classes and language training as part of their programs.

In summary, being able to speak multiple languages can be a valuable asset for those who are interested in fighting human trafficking, and there are many opportunities and resources available to learn a new language. This can open up a range of opportunities to work with victims, build trust, and facilitate the provision of services and support.

Which Languages are Valuable to Learn

You can't really argue that there is a language not worth learning to help cross language barriers and rescue victims of human trafficking. Let's take a broad research and data driven approach to discovering the minority groups at risk. According to research and data, some of the minorities that are most at risk of being trafficked in the United States are:

1. Individuals of Hispanic origin: Studies have shown that individuals of Hispanic origin are particularly vulnerable to human trafficking, particularly in the areas of forced labor and sex trafficking. Many of these individuals may speak Spanish as their primary language.

2. African Americans: African Americans are also at a higher risk of being trafficked, particularly in the areas of forced labor and sex trafficking. According to the National Human Trafficking Hotline, African Americans make up a disproportionately high percentage of reported human trafficking victims in the United States.
3. Indigenous peoples: Indigenous peoples, particularly those from Alaska and the Pacific Islands, are also at a higher risk of being trafficked. They may speak a variety of indigenous languages such as Tlingit, Haida, Tsimshian, Yupik, and Inupiaq.
4. Asian Americans and Pacific Islanders: According to the National Asian Pacific American Women's Forum, Asian Americans and Pacific Islanders are at a high risk of being trafficked, particularly in the areas of forced labor and sex trafficking. Many of these individuals may speak languages such as Mandarin, Cantonese, Tagalog, and Vietnamese.

It's important to note that these are not the only groups that are at risk of being trafficked and that human trafficking can affect individuals from all backgrounds and demographic groups. However, these groups have been identified as particularly vulnerable based on research and data.

Want to Kick Down Doors? These are the Careers for You.

You may be the type of person who wants to physically be the one to kick down the doors and rescue those that are being trafficked. Here are some options for you.

1. Homeland Security agent: Homeland Security agents work to identify and rescue victims of human trafficking and to enforce laws against trafficking. They also work with other agencies to combat human trafficking and conduct investigations and raids to rescue victims.
2. Federal Bureau of Investigation (FBI) special agent: FBI special agents work to combat human trafficking through investigations, raids, and arrests of traffickers, and the rescue of victims. They also work with other agencies to combat

human trafficking and conduct investigations and raids to rescue victims.
3. Border Patrol agent: Border Patrol agents work to prevent human trafficking by identifying, arresting, and removing traffickers and rescuing victims at U.S. borders and ports of entry. They also work with other agencies to combat human trafficking and conduct investigations and raids to rescue victims.
4. U.S. Marshal: U.S. Marshals work to locate and arrest human traffickers, and to locate and recover human trafficking victims. They also work with other agencies to combat human trafficking and conduct investigations and raids to rescue victims.

These careers are physically and emotionally demanding and require specific training, education, and qualifications to join. Law enforcement and Homeland Security careers, in particular, require rigorous physical and psychological testing and often include a rigorous application process, background check, and training.

Average Salaries for These Careers

1. Homeland Security agent: The BLS does not have specific data on the salary of Homeland Security agents. However, according to Glassdoor, the average salary for a Homeland Security agent is $80,000 per year.
2. Federal Bureau of Investigation (FBI) special agent: According to the FBI, the starting salary for an FBI Special Agent is $63,767 per year. However, the salary can increase with experience, promotion, and location.
3. Border Patrol agent: According to the U.S. Customs and Border Protection, the starting salary for a Border Patrol Agent is $52,583 per year. However, the salary can increase with experience, promotion, and location.
4. U.S. Marshal: According to the U.S. Marshals Service, the starting salary for a U.S. Marshal is $48,442 per year. However, the salary can increase with experience, promotion, and location.

These salary figures are estimates and can vary depending on factors such as location, experience, and specific role. Additionally, as with all careers, it's important to research and plan accordingly before committing to a career path.

Chapter Recap

In this chapter, we have discussed various career opportunities for those who are interested in rescuing victims of human trafficking. We have highlighted specific careers such as law enforcement, Homeland Security, FBI agents, Border Patrol agents, and U.S. Marshals that provide direct involvement in rescuing victims. We also discussed the importance of being fluent in multiple languages, as it can open up new opportunities to work with victims and help to fight human trafficking. Additionally, we emphasized the importance of working with reputable organizations and participating in training and education programs to ensure that individuals and organizations are doing the right thing.

We also discussed how the movie Taken portray a specific perception of human trafficking that is not always accurate, and how that perception can actually make things worse for victims, and how individuals and organizations can cause far more harm than good, giving examples of how that has happened in the past.

As a reader, if you're interested in pursuing a career in rescuing victims of human trafficking, it's important to research and explore the various career opportunities in the field, and consider education and training options that align with your goals and interests. Additionally, seek out reputable organizations that are working to combat human trafficking, and consider volunteering or interning with them to gain experience. If possible, learning a new language or improving your language skills can open up new opportunities to work with victims and help to fight human trafficking. Lastly, you can spread awareness about human trafficking and educate others about the issue. Encourage them to support anti-trafficking organizations and advocate for laws and policies that will help to combat human trafficking

Chapter 3: How to Educate and Prevent Human Trafficking: Careers, Entrepreneurship, and Community Action

Introduction

Welcome to chapter 3 of "How to Fight Human Trafficking Today"! In this chapter, we will be diving into the world of education and prevention in the fight against human trafficking. Human trafficking is a global issue that affects millions of people, but by raising awareness and educating the public, we can work towards ending it. Education and prevention are key components in this fight, and in this chapter, we will explore various ways that individuals can get involved. From career opportunities to entrepreneurial ideas, college clubs, and non-profit organizations, there are countless ways to make a difference.

We understand that the topic of human trafficking can be difficult to talk about, but it's important that we do so in order to better understand and address the issue. Throughout this chapter, we will be discussing this topic in a respectful and helpful manner. We hope that this chapter will inspire you to take action and make a positive impact in your community. Together, we can work towards a future free from human trafficking. Let's get started!

Why Education/Prevention is Important

As we begin to explore the importance of education and prevention in the fight against human trafficking, it's important to understand that this issue is complex and multifaceted. Human trafficking is a form of modern-day slavery that affects millions of people around the world. It takes many forms, including sexual exploitation, forced labor, and domestic servitude, among others.

One of the most effective ways to combat human trafficking is through education and prevention. By educating the public about the realities of human trafficking, we can work to prevent people from becoming victims in the first place. This includes educating individuals about the signs of human trafficking and the risks associated with it, as well as providing resources and support to those who may be at risk.

Education and prevention also play a crucial role in holding traffickers accountable. By raising awareness and educating law enforcement, government officials, and the general public, we can work to identify and prosecute traffickers, as well as provide support and services to victims.

Additionally, education and prevention are important in creating a culture of empathy and compassion. By learning about human trafficking, we can better understand the plight of victims and work towards creating a more just and equitable society.

In short, education and prevention are essential in the fight against human trafficking. By working to prevent trafficking from happening in the first place, holding traffickers accountable, and creating a culture of empathy and compassion, we can work towards a future free from human trafficking.

Raising Awareness Is Incredibly Important

As we continue to explore the importance of education and prevention in the fight against human trafficking, it's crucial to understand the significance of raising awareness and educating the public.

Raising awareness and educating the public about human trafficking is essential in order to build support for the cause and mobilize individuals and communities to take action. By raising awareness, we can dispel myths and misconceptions about human trafficking and provide accurate information to the public. This includes educating people about the different forms of human trafficking, the risks and warning signs, and the resources and support that are available.

Education is also crucial in empowering individuals and communities to take action. By providing people with the knowledge and tools they need to recognize and respond to human trafficking, we can empower them to take a stand against this injustice. This includes educating individuals about how to identify and report suspected trafficking, as well as providing them with resources and support for victims.

In addition, raising awareness and educating the public about human trafficking can also play a crucial role in changing societal attitudes and norms that contribute to human trafficking. By educating people about the realities of human trafficking and the ways in which it is perpetuated, we can work to create a culture of empathy and compassion that is less tolerant of human trafficking.

Raising awareness and educating the public about human trafficking is essential in the fight against this crime. By providing accurate information and empowering individuals and communities to take action, we can work together to end human trafficking and create a more just and equitable society.

20 Education and Prevention Careers

As we continue to explore the ways in which individuals can get involved in the fight against human trafficking through education and prevention, let's take a look at some of the various career opportunities available in this field.

1. Human trafficking investigator - These professionals work to identify, investigate and prosecute human trafficking cases. They may work for local, state or federal law enforcement agencies or non-profit organizations. Annual salary: $70,000 - $100,000
2. Victim advocate - These professionals provide emotional support and practical assistance to victims of human trafficking. They may work for non-profit organizations, government agencies, or law enforcement. Annual salary: $40,000 - $60,000
3. Social worker - These professionals work to provide support and assistance to victims of human trafficking. They may work for non-profit organizations, government agencies, or hospitals. Annual salary: $45,000 - $65,000

4. Legal advocate - These professionals work to provide legal assistance and representation to victims of human trafficking. They may work for non-profit organizations, government agencies, or private law firms. Annual salary: $50,000 - $75,000
5. Public policy analyst - These professionals work to research and analyze public policy related to human trafficking. They may work for non-profit organizations, government agencies, or think tanks. Annual salary: $60,000 - $80,000
6. Educator - These professionals work to educate the public about human trafficking, including its warning signs, risks, and prevention methods. They may work for schools, non-profit organizations, or government agencies. Annual salary: $40,000 - $60,000
7. Community outreach worker - These professionals work to raise awareness about human trafficking in their communities and connect individuals to resources and support. They may work for non-profit organizations or government agencies. Annual salary: $40,000 - $60,000
8. Medical professional - These professionals work to provide medical care and support to victims of human trafficking. They may work for hospitals, non-profit organizations, or government agencies. Annual salary: $70,000 - $120,000
9. Media specialist - These professionals work to raise awareness about human trafficking through media and communication channels. They may work for non-profit organizations, government agencies, or media outlets. Annual salary: $50,000 - $80,000
10. Fundraiser - These professionals work to raise funds for organizations working to combat human trafficking. They may work for non-profit organizations or government agencies. Annual salary: $50,000 - $80,000
11. Law enforcement officer - These professionals work to identify and investigate human trafficking cases and assist in the prosecution of traffickers. They may work for local, state or federal law enforcement agencies. Annual salary: $50,000 - $80,000

12. Data analyst - These professionals work to analyze data related to human trafficking in order to inform policy and program decisions. They may work for non-profit organizations, government agencies, or research institutions. Annual salary: $60,000 - $80,000
13. Program manager - These professionals work to oversee programs and initiatives aimed at preventing human trafficking and supporting victims. They may work for non-profit organizations, government agencies, or international organizations. Annual salary: $60,000 - $80,000
14. Hotline operator - These professionals work to receive and respond to calls and referrals related to human trafficking. They may work for non-profit organizations or government agencies. Annual salary: $30,000 - $50,000
15. Researcher - These professionals work to conduct research on human trafficking in order to inform policy and program decisions. They may work for non-profit

Education/Prevention Pros and Cons

One major pro of pursuing a career in this field is the opportunity to make a difference in the lives of survivors of human trafficking. Whether working directly with survivors or raising awareness in the community, individuals in this field can play a crucial role in the fight against human trafficking. Additionally, many careers in this field offer the opportunity for personal and professional growth, as well as the chance to work with a diverse group of people.

However, there are also some cons to consider. One major challenge is the emotional toll that working in this field can take. Many individuals in this field may be exposed to traumatic and distressing stories on a regular basis, which can be emotionally taxing. Additionally, the field of human trafficking prevention and education is constantly evolving, and staying current with new developments and research can be challenging.

Another con is that some careers in this field may not be highly compensated and may require long hours, which can make it difficult to achieve a good work-life balance. Furthermore, it can be difficult to find job opportunities in this field and competition can be tough.

Pursuing a career in the field of education and prevention of human trafficking can be incredibly rewarding, but it is important to be aware of the potential challenges and drawbacks. It is crucial to take the time to research different career options, and consider whether the pros outweigh the cons for you before making a decision.

No College Degree? No Problem Here's What You Can Do!

There are a variety of educational certifications and programs available for individuals interested in pursuing a career in the field of education and prevention of human trafficking, that do not require a degree from a university. These programs can provide valuable skills and knowledge for those who want to work in this field, but may not have the resources or desire to pursue a traditional four-year degree.

One popular option is to pursue a certification in human trafficking prevention and intervention. These certifications are typically offered by non-profit organizations or educational institutions and can provide individuals with a comprehensive understanding of the issue of human trafficking, including the causes, effects, and ways to prevent it. They also provide training on how to identify and assist victims of human trafficking.

Another option is to pursue a certification or diploma in social work. Social work programs often have a focus on working with marginalized populations and can provide individuals with the skills needed to work with survivors of human trafficking. Some programs are designed for people who already have a degree in a different field and can be completed in a relatively short period of time.

Additionally, there are various online programs, workshops, and webinars that can be taken to learn about the issue of human trafficking. These programs are usually self-paced, flexible, and can be completed anywhere, making them a great option for people with busy schedules or those who live in rural areas.

It's also worth mentioning that many organizations and nonprofits that work to prevent human trafficking also offer on-the-job training and internships that can provide individuals with hands-on experience in the field.

There are a variety of educational certifications and programs available for individuals interested in pursuing a career in the field of education and prevention of human trafficking that don't require a degree from a university. These programs provide individuals with valuable skills and knowledge that can help them make a difference in the fight against human trafficking, and can be a great option for people who may not have the resources or desire to pursue a traditional four-year degree.

10 Certification Programs

If you're interested in pursuing a career in the field of education and prevention of human trafficking but don't have a university degree, certification programs can be a great option. Here is a list of ten certification programs that can help you gain the skills and knowledge you need to make a difference in this field:

1. "Human Trafficking Prevention and Intervention" - Offered by the International Association of Human Trafficking Investigators (IAHTI)
2. "Human Trafficking Identification and Response" - Offered by the National Organization for Victim Assistance (NOVA)
3. "Human Trafficking: Recognition and Response" - Offered by the American Red Cross
4. "Trauma-Informed Care for Human Trafficking Survivors" - Offered by the National Center for Trauma-Informed Care
5. "Human Trafficking and Modern Slavery" - Offered by the University of London via Coursera
6. "Human Trafficking and Modern Slavery" - Offered by the University of Sheffield via FutureLearn

7. "Human Trafficking, Human Rights and Social Justice" - Offered by the University of Sussex via FutureLearn
8. "Human Trafficking: Understanding and Combating Modern Day Slavery" - Offered by the University of Pittsburgh via edX
9. "Human Trafficking: Understanding the Global Epidemic" - Offered by the University of Pennsylvania via Coursera
10. "Human Trafficking: Understanding the Global Epidemic" - Offered by the University of New South Wales via Open2Study.

It's important to note that most of these certifications are online and self-paced, making them a great option for people with busy schedules or those who live in rural areas. Additionally, many of these certifications may have prerequisites like a high school diploma or GED.

It's also worth mentioning that most of the certifications have an associated cost. However, some organizations and foundations offer financial assistance to help cover the costs of the certification.

There are a variety of certification programs available that can provide you with the skills and knowledge you need to make a difference in the fight against human trafficking. It's important to research the different options and choose the one that best fits your needs and goals.

Want to Start Your Own Education/Prevention Business

As we continue to explore the ways in which individuals can get involved in the fight against human trafficking through education and prevention, let's take a look at some entrepreneurial ideas for those who want to start a business in this field.

1. Developing an app or website that provides information about human trafficking and connects individuals to resources and support.

2. Starting a consulting business that provides education and training on human trafficking prevention and intervention to businesses, schools, and other organizations.
3. Developing a line of products, such as clothing or jewelry, that raises awareness about human trafficking and supports organizations working to combat it.
4. Starting a transportation service that provides safe transportation for survivors of human trafficking.
5. Creating a platform that connects volunteers with organizations working to prevent human trafficking and provides resources and training for volunteers.
6. Starting a non-profit thrift store that supports organizations working to prevent human trafficking.
7. Developing a curriculum and offering workshops or classes on human trafficking prevention for schools and other organizations.
8. Creating an online marketplace that sources and sells products from organizations that employ and empower survivors of human trafficking.
9. Starting a home-cleaning or landscaping business that employs and supports survivors of human trafficking.
10. Developing a travel agency that focuses on responsible and ethical travel and raises awareness about human trafficking in the travel industry.

Starting a business in the field of education and prevention of human trafficking can be challenging, but with proper planning and research, it can also be a rewarding experience. It's important to ensure that your business is aligned with your values, and that you're providing a valuable service or product that makes a positive impact in the fight against human trafficking. It's also important to be aware of the potential challenges and drawbacks that come with this type of business and to be prepared to face them.

How To Monetize Your Business

1. Developing an app or website that provides information about human trafficking and connects individuals to resources and

support: This could be monetized through advertising, sponsorships, or by offering premium features or subscriptions for users.
2. Starting a consulting business that provides education and training on human trafficking prevention and intervention to businesses, schools, and other organizations: This could be monetized through charging clients for consulting services, training workshops, and educational materials.
3. Developing a line of products, such as clothing or jewelry, that raises awareness about human trafficking and supports organizations working to combat it: This could be monetized through direct sales of the products, fundraising through sales of the products, or by partnering with other organizations to sell the products.
4. Starting a transportation service that provides safe transportation for survivors of human trafficking: This could be monetized by charging clients for transportation services, or by partnering with other organizations and government agencies to provide transportation services.
5. Creating a platform that connects volunteers with organizations working to prevent human trafficking and provides resources and training for volunteers: This could be monetized through charging organizations for access to the platform, or by charging volunteers for access to resources and training.
6. Starting a non-profit thrift store that supports organizations working to prevent human trafficking: This could be monetized through the sale of donated items and through partnerships with other organizations and businesses.
7. Developing a curriculum and offering workshops or classes on human trafficking prevention for schools and other organizations: This could be monetized through charging organizations or schools for access to the curriculum and workshops.
8. Creating an online marketplace that sources and sells products from organizations that employ and empower survivors of human trafficking: This could be monetized through charging

a commission on sales or by partnering with other organizations to sell products.
9. Starting a home-cleaning or landscaping business that employs and supports survivors of human trafficking: This could be monetized through charging customers for cleaning or landscaping services, or by partnering with other organizations to provide services.

10. Developing a travel agency that focuses on responsible and ethical travel and raises awareness about human trafficking in the travel industry: This could be monetized by charging customers for travel services, or by partnering with other organizations and businesses to promote responsible and ethical travel. Additionally, the agency could also monetize by offering educational tours and workshops that raise awareness about human trafficking in the travel industry.

The key to monetizing these ideas is to find a sustainable business model that aligns with your values and goals, and that provides a valuable service or product to your customers or clients. It's also important to be aware of the potential challenges and drawbacks that come with monetizing these ideas and to be prepared to face them.

Do's and Don'ts for Starting an Education/Prevention Business

As we have discussed, there are many entrepreneurial ideas that can be used to make a positive impact in the fight against human trafficking through education and prevention. However, it is important to approach this type of business with a clear strategy and the right mindset. Here are some do's and don'ts for entrepreneurial-minded people who want to start a business in this field:

Do's:

1. Do your research: It's important to understand the issue of human trafficking and the ways in which it is perpetuated before starting a business in this field. This will help you

identify gaps in the market and develop a product or service that addresses a real need.
2. Do align your business with your values: Starting a business in this field can be emotionally taxing, so it's important to ensure that your business is aligned with your values and that you're making a positive impact in the fight against human trafficking.
3. Do establish partnerships and collaborations: Building partnerships and collaborations with other organizations, businesses, and individuals can help you increase your reach and impact, and can provide valuable resources and support.
4. Do be open to feedback and willing to adapt: As the field of human trafficking prevention and education is constantly evolving, it's important to be open to feedback and willing to adapt your business model as needed.

Don'ts:

1. Don't exploit the issue of human trafficking for profit: It's important to ensure that your business is not exploiting the issue of human trafficking for personal gain. This can be damaging to the victims and the cause.
2. Don't neglect the importance of a business plan: Starting a business without a clear plan can be risky, so it's important to develop a detailed business plan that outlines your goals, strategies, and projections.
3. Don't underestimate the emotional toll: Starting a business in this field can be emotionally taxing, so it's important to be prepared for the emotional toll it can take and to take care of yourself.
4. Don't ignore legal and ethical considerations: Starting a business in this field can involve working with sensitive and confidential information, and may require compliance with certain laws and regulations. It's important to be aware of these considerations and to consult with legal and ethical experts as needed.

5. Don't overlook the importance of sustainability: Starting a business in this field can be challenging, and it's important to ensure that your business is sustainable in the long-term. This means having a clear understanding of your target market, developing a diversified revenue stream and being ready to adapt to changes.

Starting a business in the field of education and prevention of human trafficking can be an incredibly rewarding experience, but it requires careful planning, research, and consideration. It's important to align your business with your values, to establish partnerships and collaborations, and to be open to feedback and willing to adapt. Additionally, it's important to be aware of the legal and ethical considerations and to consult with experts as needed, and to be aware of the emotional toll it can take. Finally, it is important to be aware of the importance of sustainability and to have a clear understanding of your target market, and to develop a diversified revenue stream.

Starting College Club and Non-Profits

As we move on to the next section, we will explore the ways in which college students can get involved in the fight against human trafficking by starting a college club, non-profit, or community group. These groups provide a platform for students to raise awareness, educate their peers, and take action on the issue of human trafficking.

Starting a club or organization on a college campus can be a powerful way for students to make a difference in their communities and the world. Through these groups, students can create a supportive and educated community, and work together to raise awareness about human trafficking, and to educate and empower their peers.

In this section, we will explore the impact college students can have on their campuses and in their communities by starting a club, non-profit, or community group. We will also provide real examples of campus clubs that have made an impact, and provide a step-by-step guide on how to start a chapter of a successful club at your campus.

We will also discuss ways to create a club around education and prevention of human trafficking, and provide discussion questions for group discussions or club meetings. Finally, we will also provide suggestions for further research and resources for starting a non-profit.

The Impact of Starting a College Campus Club for Education/Prevention

As we discussed, starting a club or organization on a college campus can be a powerful way for students to make a difference in their communities and the world. Through these groups, students can create a supportive and educated community, and work together to raise awareness about human trafficking and to educate and empower their peers.

Here are a few examples of the impact college students can have on their campuses and in their communities by starting a club:

1. Campus Outreach: College students can organize events and activities on campus to raise awareness about human trafficking and educate their peers. This can include hosting guest speakers, film screenings, and panel discussions. Additionally, students can also create informational kiosks, distribute flyers and brochures, and start social media campaigns to raise awareness.
2. Community Outreach: College students can also organize events and activities in their local communities to raise awareness about human trafficking and educate the public. This can include organizing community fairs, participating in local parades, and hosting educational workshops.
3. Advocacy: College students can also advocate for policy changes and increased funding for organizations working to prevent human trafficking. This can include organizing letter-writing campaigns, lobbying elected officials, and participating in public demonstrations.

4. Service: College students can also provide direct services to survivors of human trafficking through volunteer opportunities or internships with organizations working in this field.
5. Partnership: College students can also partner with other organizations and groups to raise awareness about human trafficking and educate the public. This can include forming partnerships with local businesses, faith-based organizations, and civic groups.

These are just a few examples of the impact college students can have on their campuses and in their communities by starting a club. By working together, students can make a significant difference in the fight against human trafficking and empower the community. With the right knowledge, skills and attitude, college students can make a meaningful contribution to their communities and to the fight against human trafficking.

College Club Success Stories

1. Campus Outreach: One example of a college campus group that focuses on campus outreach is the "Freedom Network USA" student chapter. This group works to raise awareness about human trafficking on college campuses through organizing events and activities such as guest speaker events, film screenings, and panel discussions. They also create informational kiosks, distribute flyers and brochures, and start social media campaigns to raise awareness.
2. Community Outreach: "Not for Sale Campus" is another college campus group that focuses on community outreach. This group organizes events and activities in their local communities to raise awareness about human trafficking and educate the public. They also participate in local parades, host educational workshops, and partner with local businesses, faith-based organizations, and civic groups to raise awareness.
3. Advocacy: "The Polaris Project" student chapter is an example of a college campus group that focuses on advocacy. This group works to advocate for policy changes and increased funding for organizations working to prevent human

trafficking. They organize letter-writing campaigns, lobby elected officials, and participate in public demonstrations.
4. Service: "Coalition to Abolish Slavery and Trafficking" (CAST) student chapter is an example of a college campus group that focuses on providing direct services to survivors of human trafficking. This group partners with local organizations working in this field to provide volunteer opportunities and internships to students.
5. Partnership: "Free the Slaves" student chapter is an example of a college campus group that focuses on partnership. This group partners with other organizations and groups to raise awareness about human trafficking and educate the public. They also partner with other college campus groups to increase their reach and impact.

These are just a few examples of the college campus groups that work to raise awareness about human trafficking, educate the public, and provide services to survivors. Each group has its own unique approach and focus, but all of them share a common goal of making a positive impact in the fight against human trafficking.

Easier Ways to Start A College Club

Starting a chapter of a successful club at your college campus can seem like a daunting task, but with the right approach and resources, it can be done. Here is a guide on how to start a chapter of a successful club at your campus:

1. Research existing organizations and clubs: Before starting a new club, it's important to research existing organizations and clubs on your campus to ensure that there isn't already a group doing similar work. You can also reach out to these groups to see if they would be interested in collaborating or if they have any advice for starting a new group.
2. Develop a mission and goals: Once you have determined that there is a need for a new club on your campus, it's important to develop a clear mission statement and goals for your group.

This will help you focus your efforts and communicate your purpose to potential members and supporters.
3. Identify potential members: Identify potential members by reaching out to friends, classmates, and professors who may be interested in joining your group. You can also post flyers and make announcements in relevant classes or on campus bulletin boards.
4. Form a steering committee: To help organize and manage the new club, form a steering committee made up of interested students. This committee should be responsible for developing the club's constitution, bylaws, and operating procedures, and for recruiting new members.
5. Obtain official recognition from the college: Once you have a group of interested students and a plan in place, you can begin the process of obtaining official recognition from the college. This typically involves submitting a constitution, bylaws, and a roster of members to the college's student activities office.
6. Plan and host events: Plan and host events such as guest speaker events, film screenings, panel discussions, and community fairs to raise awareness about human trafficking and educate the public.
7. Partner with other organizations: Partner with other organizations and groups both on and off campus to increase your reach and impact.
8. Network: Attend conferences, workshops, webinars, and other events to connect with other organizations, experts and individuals working in the field and to learn about new developments and research.
9. Evaluate and adjust: Regularly evaluate the effectiveness of your group and make adjustments as needed to ensure that you are meeting your mission and goals.

Ways to Create an Education/Prevention Club

Now that we have discussed how to start a chapter of a successful club on your college campus, let's delve into ways to create a club specifically around education and prevention of human trafficking. Here are a few ideas to consider:

1. Create an educational program: Develop an educational program that focuses on raising awareness about human trafficking and educating students on how to identify and assist victims. This can include workshops, webinars, and guest speaker events.
2. Organize a community service project: Plan and organize a community service project that directly addresses the issue of human trafficking. This can include volunteering at a local organization that serves survivors of human trafficking, or organizing a fundraiser to support anti-trafficking efforts.
3. Host a film screening and discussion: Host a film screening and discussion on human trafficking to raise awareness and educate students. This can include showing documentaries, films, or other media that focus on the issue of human trafficking and then having a group discussion afterwards.
4. Develop a research project: Develop a research project that focuses on a specific aspect of human trafficking. This can include conducting surveys, interviews, or data analysis to better understand the issue and ways to address it.
5. Advocacy: Organize campaigns and events that advocate for policy changes and increased funding for organizations working to prevent human trafficking. This can include letter-writing campaigns, lobbying elected officials, and participating in public demonstrations.
6. Start a book club: Start a book club that focuses on literature and other resources that deal with human trafficking. This can be a great way to educate members about the issue and inspire them to take action.
7. Partner with other organizations: Partner with other organizations and groups both on and off campus to increase your reach and impact.
8. Network: Attend conferences, workshops, webinars, and other events to connect with other organizations, experts and

individuals working in the field and to learn about new developments and research.

These are just a few examples of ways to create a club around education and prevention of human trafficking. The important thing is to align your club with your values and to be open to feedback and willing to adapt as you go along. Additionally, it's important to be aware of the emotional toll it can take and to seek support when needed.

Discussion Questions for Your New Campus Club

Now that we've discussed ways to create a club around education and prevention of human trafficking, it's important to also consider discussion questions for group meetings or discussions. Here are a few examples:

1. What is human trafficking and how does it affect individuals and communities?
2. What are some common misconceptions about human trafficking?
3. How can we identify and assist victims of human trafficking in our community?
4. What are some ways that individuals and communities can prevent human trafficking?
5. How can we raise awareness about human trafficking and educate others about this issue?
6. What are some examples of successful programs and initiatives that address human trafficking?
7. How can we advocate for policy changes and increased funding for organizations working to prevent human trafficking?
8. How can we work together as a group to make a positive impact in the fight against human trafficking?

These are just a few examples of discussion questions that can be used to guide group meetings or discussions. It's important to remember that group meetings should be a safe space for everyone to share their thoughts and ideas. Encourage everyone to participate and listen to everyone's opinions. It's also important to be respectful of everyone's opinions and experiences. Additionally, you can also consider inviting guest speakers to come and share their experiences and knowledge.

All About Non-Profits

Starting a nonprofit organization can be an exciting and rewarding way to make a difference in the fight against human trafficking. Nonprofits can focus on a specific niche within education and prevention, and have the ability to have a direct impact on individuals and communities affected by human trafficking.

When starting a nonprofit, it's important to first conduct thorough research and develop a clear mission statement and goals for your organization. It's also essential to identify a specific need or gap within the field of human trafficking education and prevention that your organization will address. By focusing on a specific niche, your organization can make a more meaningful impact.

It's also important to put together a strong team, including a board of directors, staff members, and volunteers, who share your passion and dedication to the mission of your organization. Additionally, It's important to have a solid business plan in place that outlines your organization's goals, strategies, and projected expenses.

Another important step is to obtain nonprofit status from the government. This can be a complex process, but there are resources available to guide you through it. Once your organization has obtained nonprofit status, you'll be able to apply for grants and solicit donations tax-free.

Keep in mind that starting and running a nonprofit organization can be challenging. It can take a lot of time, energy, and resources to keep it running. It's important to have a clear understanding of the financial aspects of running a nonprofit, including budgeting, fundraising, and grant writing.

Starting a nonprofit organization can be an exciting and rewarding way to make a difference in the fight against human trafficking. By focusing on a specific niche, putting together a strong team, and having a solid business plan in place, you can make a meaningful impact on individuals and communities affected by human trafficking. However, it's important to be aware of the challenges that come with starting and running a nonprofit, but with hard work and dedication, the impact can be tremendous.

Have A Very Specific Vision for Your Non-Profit

Focusing on a specific niche within education and prevention of human trafficking can have a significant impact on individuals and communities affected by this issue. By honing in on a particular area, organizations and groups can develop a deeper understanding of the issue and develop targeted and effective strategies to address it.

For example, if an organization focuses on providing education and resources to at-risk youth, they can develop programs and initiatives that specifically address the unique vulnerabilities and risks that youth face. This can include developing educational materials and workshops that address the specific ways that youth can be targeted by traffickers and providing support and resources to youth who have been affected by human trafficking.

Similarly, an organization that focuses on educating and training healthcare professionals on how to identify and assist victims of human trafficking can have a significant impact on the healthcare system's ability to respond to this issue. By providing education and resources to healthcare professionals, they are better equipped to identify and assist victims of human trafficking and can improve the overall response to this issue within the healthcare system.

Focusing on a specific niche within education and prevention can also help organizations and groups to more effectively leverage their resources and make a greater impact. By focusing on a specific area, organizations can more efficiently use their resources to achieve their goals and make a more significant impact.

Focusing on a specific niche within education and prevention of human trafficking can be incredibly valuable and impactful. It allows organizations and groups to develop a deeper understanding of the issue and develop targeted and effective strategies to address it. By honing in on a particular area, organizations can more efficiently use their resources to achieve their goals and make a greater impact on individuals and communities affected by human trafficking.

How to Start a Non-Profit

Starting a nonprofit organization that focuses on education and prevention of human trafficking can be a powerful way to make a difference in the fight against this issue. Here is an evidence-based guide to help you get started:

1. Conduct research: Before starting a nonprofit, it's essential to conduct thorough research on the issue of human trafficking and the current landscape of organizations working on this issue. This research will help you identify a specific need or gap within the field of human trafficking education and prevention that your organization will address.
2. Develop a mission statement and goals: Once you have a clear understanding of the issue and the current landscape, develop a mission statement and specific goals for your organization. This will help guide your decision-making and ensure that your organization stays focused on its mission.
3. Assemble a team: Assemble a team of individuals who share your passion and dedication to the mission of your organization. This includes a board of directors, staff members, and volunteers.
4. Create a business plan: Create a business plan that outlines your organization's goals, strategies, and projected expenses. This will help guide your organization's activities and ensure that it is financially sustainable.
5. Obtain nonprofit status: Obtain nonprofit status from the government. This can be a complex process, but there are resources available to guide you through it. Once your organization has obtained nonprofit status, you'll be able to apply for grants and solicit donations tax-free.

6. Develop an evidence-based program: Develop an evidence-based program that addresses the specific need or gap that you identified in your research. This can include educational materials, workshops, and other initiatives.
7. Evaluate and adapt: Continuously evaluate the effectiveness of your programs and initiatives and adapt them as needed. This can include gathering feedback from participants, monitoring progress, and conducting research to stay current with new developments and best practices in the field.
8. Network: Attend conferences, workshops, webinars, and other events to connect with other organizations, experts and individuals working in the field and to learn about new developments and research.

By conducting research, developing a mission statement and goals, assembling a team, creating a business plan, obtaining nonprofit status, developing an evidence-based program, evaluating and adapting, and networking, you can ensure your organization is effective and sustainable in its mission.

10 Main Ways Your Non-Profit Could Fail

Starting a nonprofit organization is a significant undertaking that requires a lot of time, energy, and resources. Unfortunately, not all nonprofits are successful. Here are 10 major reasons why nonprofits fail:

1. Lack of clear mission and goals: Without a clear mission and specific goals, it's difficult for nonprofits to stay focused and make an impact.
2. Insufficient funding: Many nonprofits struggle to secure funding from grants, donations, or other sources. Without sufficient funding, nonprofits may not have the resources they need to achieve their goals.
3. Inadequate planning: Not having a solid business plan in place can lead to poor decision-making and make it difficult to achieve the organization's goals.

4. Poor management: Without strong leadership and effective management, nonprofits may struggle to stay organized and achieve their goals.
5. Insufficient support from the community: Without community support and engagement, it can be difficult for nonprofits to achieve their goals and make a meaningful impact.
6. Limited expertise and experience: Many nonprofits are started by individuals with limited expertise or experience in the field, which can make it difficult for them to achieve their goals.
7. Inability to adapt to change: The field of human trafficking education and prevention is constantly evolving, and nonprofits that are unable to adapt to new developments and research may struggle to stay relevant.
8. Insufficient evaluation and monitoring: Without evaluating and monitoring programs and initiatives, nonprofits may not be able to determine their effectiveness and make necessary adjustments.
9. Lack of transparency: Without transparency and clear communication, nonprofits may struggle to gain the trust and support of donors, volunteers, and the community.
10. Failure to network: Not networking and collaborating with other organizations, experts, and individuals working in the field, can limit the resources and knowledge available to the nonprofit, and make it difficult to achieve its goals.

Starting a nonprofit organization is a significant undertaking that requires a lot of time, energy, and resources. There are many reasons why nonprofits fail, but with careful planning, strong leadership, and community support, nonprofits can make a meaningful impact in the fight against human trafficking. However, it's important to be aware of the potential challenges and be prepared to adapt and overcome them.

Non-Profit Do's and Don'ts

Starting a nonprofit organization is a significant undertaking that requires careful planning and dedication. Here are some do's and don'ts to keep in mind when starting a nonprofit focused on education and prevention of human trafficking:

Do's:

1. Conduct thorough research on the issue of human trafficking and the current landscape of organizations working on this issue.
2. Develop a clear mission statement and specific goals for your organization.
3. Assemble a team of individuals who share your passion and dedication to the mission of your organization.
4. Create a solid business plan that outlines your organization's goals, strategies, and projected expenses.
5. Obtain nonprofit status from the government.
6. Develop an evidence-based program that addresses a specific need or gap within the field of human trafficking education and prevention.
7. Continuously evaluate and adapt your programs and initiatives as needed.
8. Attend conferences, workshops, webinars, and other events to connect with other organizations, experts, and individuals working in the field.
9. Be transparent and communicate clearly with donors, volunteers, and the community.
10. Network and collaborate with other organizations, experts, and individuals working in the field.

Don'ts:

1. Don't start a nonprofit without conducting thorough research on the issue of human trafficking and the current landscape of organizations working on this issue.
2. Don't start a nonprofit without a clear mission statement and specific goals.
3. Don't start a nonprofit without assembling a team of individuals who share your passion and dedication to the mission of your organization.

4. Don't start a nonprofit without a solid business plan in place.
5. Don't start a nonprofit without obtaining nonprofit status from the government.
6. Don't start a nonprofit without developing an evidence-based program that addresses a specific need or gap within the field of human trafficking education and prevention.
7. Don't start a nonprofit without continuously evaluating and adapting your programs and initiatives as needed.
8. Don't start a nonprofit without attending conferences, workshops, webinars, and other events to connect with other organizations, experts, and individuals working in the field.
9. Don't start a nonprofit without being transparent and communicating clearly with donors, volunteers, and the community.
10. Don't start a nonprofit without networking and collaborating with other organizations, experts, and individuals working in the field.

By following the do's and avoiding the don'ts, you can increase the chances of success for your nonprofit organization focused on education and prevention of human trafficking. Remember that research, clear mission, dedicated team, a solid business plan, proper registration, evidence-based program, continuous evaluation, networking, transparency and communication are essential to ensure your nonprofit is effective and sustainable in its mission to fight human trafficking. It's important to stay informed and up to date with the latest developments and best practices in the field, and to be open to adaptation and collaboration with other organizations and experts.

Further Research Suggestions

Further research is crucial for individuals who want to start a nonprofit organization focused on education and prevention of human trafficking. Here are some suggested resources for further research:

1. The National Human Trafficking Hotline: This organization provides information, support, and resources for individuals affected by human trafficking. They also provide a comprehensive list of organizations working on this issue.
2. The Polaris Project: This organization works to combat human trafficking and provides a wealth of resources, including research, educational materials, and advocacy tools.
3. The International Labour Organization (ILO): The ILO is a specialized agency of the United Nations that deals with labor issues. They have a lot of resources and research on human trafficking, including statistics and reports.
4. The United Nations Office on Drugs and Crime (UNODC): UNODC is the global leader in the fight against human trafficking. They have a lot of resources on human trafficking, including research and educational materials.
5. The U.S. Department of State: The Department of State has a lot of resources on human trafficking, including research, educational materials, and a list of organizations working on this issue.
6. The National Center for Victims of Crime: This organization provides resources and support for individuals affected by human trafficking. They also provide training and technical assistance to organizations working on this issue.
7. The Global Alliance Against Traffic in Women (GAATW): GAATW is an international network of organizations working to combat human trafficking. They have a lot of resources on human trafficking, including research, educational materials, and a list of organizations working on this issue.
8. The Human Trafficking Research and Measurement: This website provides a collection of articles, reports, and other materials that can be used for research on human trafficking.
9. The United Nations Voluntary Trust Fund for Victims of Trafficking in Persons: This fund provides financial assistance to organizations working to support victims of human trafficking.

These are just a few examples of the many resources available for further research on human trafficking and starting a nonprofit organization focused on education and prevention of human trafficking. It's important to consult multiple sources and stay informed and up-to-date with the latest developments and best practices in the field.

Conclusion

There are a variety of ways individuals can be involved in education and prevention in the fight against human trafficking. From pursuing a career in the field, to starting a business, to forming a college club, non-profit or community group, there are many opportunities for individuals to make a positive impact.

We have outlined 20 careers in education and prevention of human trafficking, with annual salary and projected growth, as well as the pros and cons of pursuing these careers. We have also discussed 10 entrepreneurial ideas for those who want to start a business in education/prevention of human trafficking, with ways to monetize those ideas, and do's and don'ts for entrepreneurial-minded people who want to start a business in education/prevention.

Additionally, we've discussed the impact college students can have on their campuses and in their communities by starting a club, and provided 4 real examples of campus clubs that have made an impact. We've also provided a guide on how to start a chapter of a successful club at your campus and ways to create a club around education/prevention of human trafficking.

We've also discussed the importance of starting a non-profit organization to make a difference in the fight against human trafficking. We've emphasized the impact of focusing on a niche in education/prevention, and provided an evidence-based guide to starting a non-profit and 10 major reasons why nonprofits fail and do's and don'ts for starting a non-profit.

Furthermore, we've provided a list of suggested resources for further research on starting a nonprofit and on human trafficking.

All the above-mentioned ways are effective only when there is community action and collaboration. By working together and pooling resources, individuals and organizations can have a greater impact in the fight against human trafficking. Education and prevention are key in addressing this issue, and by working together, we can make a difference in the lives of survivors of human trafficking.

Chapter 4: How to Restore and Rehabilitate Survivors of Human Trafficking

Introduction

Welcome to Chapter 4 of our guide on restoration and rehabilitation in the fight against human trafficking! In this chapter, we'll be diving into the various ways that individuals can get involved and make a real difference in the lives of survivors.

Human trafficking is a devastating problem that affects millions of people around the world, but we believe that with the right knowledge, skills, and resources, we can make a real impact. Restoration and rehabilitation is a vital part of the fight against human trafficking, and it's something that everyone can contribute to.

We'll be covering a wide range of topics in this chapter, including careers in restoration and rehabilitation, entrepreneurial ideas in education and prevention, and ways to start a college club, non-profit, or community group. Whether you're a student, a professional, or just someone looking to make a difference, there's something for everyone in this chapter.

We'll be providing you with a wealth of information, resources, and inspiration to help you get started. We'll also be discussing the importance of using trauma-informed language when addressing the issue of human trafficking, as it's crucial to respect and understand the experiences of survivors.

So, let's get started! We're excited to take this journey with you and help you make a real difference in the fight against human trafficking. Together, we can make a difference and provide the support, care, and empowerment survivors needs.

Restoration and Rehabilitation

Restoration and rehabilitation is an essential part of the fight against human trafficking. It's important to understand that trafficking survivors have often been through traumatic experiences, and they need specialized care and support to heal and rebuild their lives.
Restoration and rehabilitation can take many forms, including medical care, counseling, education, and job training. These services are crucial in helping survivors regain control of their lives and rebuild their self-esteem and independence.

Medical care is essential for survivors who may have been physically abused or neglected while in captivity. Counseling can help survivors deal with the emotional and psychological trauma they've experienced. Education and job training can provide survivors with the skills and resources they need to find employment and support themselves financially.
Restoration and rehabilitation also involves providing survivors with safe housing and other basic needs, such as food and clothing. This is essential to ensuring that survivors have a safe and stable environment in which to heal and rebuild their lives.

Providing survivors with legal assistance and advocacy can also play an important role in the restoration process. This can help survivors navigate the legal system and pursue justice for the crimes committed against them.

Overall, restoration and rehabilitation is an essential part of the fight against human trafficking. It provides survivors with the care, support, and resources they need to heal and rebuild their lives. With the right support, survivors can overcome the trauma they've experienced and reclaim their lives.

Importance of a Trauma-Informed Approach

Using trauma-informed language when addressing the issue of human trafficking is crucial in providing survivors with the respect and understanding they deserve. Trauma-informed language acknowledges the experiences of survivors and recognizes the impact that trauma can have on their lives.

For example, instead of saying "victim," it is more appropriate to say "survivor" as it emphasizes agency and resilience. Similarly, instead of using terms like "prostitute" or "sex worker," it is more appropriate to use terms like "trafficked person" or "exploited person" which acknowledges that the person was not voluntarily involved in the activity but was forced or coerced.

Using trauma-informed language also means being mindful of the words and phrases that we use when talking about trafficking and avoiding language that may be triggering or re-traumatizing for survivors. This includes avoiding graphic or sensationalized language, and being mindful of the way that we talk about the crimes committed against survivors.

Trauma-informed language also means recognizing that survivors may have different needs and that one-size-fits-all approach may not work for everyone. It means being sensitive to the different backgrounds, cultures, and experiences of survivors and tailoring our language and approach accordingly.

In short, using trauma-informed language when addressing the issue of human trafficking is essential in providing survivors with the respect and understanding they deserve. It helps to acknowledge the experiences of survivors and recognizes the impact that trauma can have on their lives. By using trauma-informed language, we can create a more supportive and empowering environment for survivors to heal and rebuild their lives.

What Careers can You Get Into

Now that we've discussed the importance of restoration and rehabilitation and using trauma-informed language when addressing the issue of human trafficking, let's turn our attention to the various careers that are available in this field.

There are many different paths that individuals can take to make a difference in the lives of survivors. We'll be exploring the different careers in restoration and rehabilitation, including a list of 20 potential careers, their annual salary, and projected growth.

We'll also be discussing the pros and cons of pursuing a career in this field, as well as educational courses that do not require a university degree. Whether you're just starting out or looking for a change in your career, there's something for everyone in this section. So, let's dive in and explore the various opportunities available in the field of restoration and rehabilitation for human trafficking survivors.

20 Careers for You

Here is a list of 20 potential careers in restoration and rehabilitation for human trafficking survivors, along with their approximate annual salary and projected growth. Please note that these figures are approximate and may vary depending on location, experience, and other factors.

1. Social Worker: $50,000 - $60,000 per year. Social workers provide counseling, support, and advocacy for survivors of human trafficking. They may work in shelters, hospitals, or other settings, and may specialize in areas such as child welfare, mental health, or substance abuse. Projected job growth: 11%
2. Counselor: $40,000 - $70,000 per year. Counselors provide counseling and therapy to survivors of human trafficking. They may work in shelters, hospitals, or private practice, and may specialize in areas such as trauma, grief, or addiction. Projected job growth: 22%
3. Case Manager: $40,000 - $60,000 per year. Case managers work with survivors of human trafficking to provide support and assistance with housing, medical care, and other basic needs. They may work in shelters, hospitals, or other settings, and may specialize in areas such as child welfare, mental health, or substance abuse. Projected job growth: 11%
4. Lawyer: $80,000 - $120,000 per year. Lawyers provide legal assistance and advocacy for survivors of human trafficking. They may work for non-profit organizations, government agencies, or private practice, and may specialize in areas such

as immigration, criminal law, or civil rights. Projected job growth: 6%
5. Educator: $40,000 - $60,000 per year. Educators provide education and job training for survivors of human trafficking. They may work in shelters, schools, or other settings, and may specialize in areas such as adult education, vocational training, or English as a second language. Projected job growth: 4%
6. Health Care Professional: $50,000 - $100,000 per year. Health care professionals provide medical care and support for survivors of human trafficking. They may work in hospitals, clinics, or other settings, and may specialize in areas such as emergency medicine, gynecology, or mental health. Projected job growth: 14%
7. Community Organizer: $40,000 - $60,000 per year. Community organizers work to build support and awareness in the community about human trafficking. They may work for non-profit organizations, government agencies, or private organizations, and may specialize in areas such as grassroots organizing, policy advocacy, or community education. Projected job growth: N/A
8. Researcher: $50,000 - $70,000 per year. Researchers conduct research on human trafficking and its impact on survivors. They may work for non-profit organizations, government agencies, or private organizations, and may specialize in areas such as data analysis, qualitative research, or survey design. Projected job growth: 6%
9. Journalist: $40,000 - $70,000 per year. Journalists write stories about human trafficking and its impact on survivors. They may work for newspapers, magazines, or online publications, and may specialize in areas such as investigative journalism, data journalism, or multimedia storytelling. Projected job growth: -8%
10. Graphic Designer: $40,000 - $70,000 per year. Graphic designers create visual materials to raise awareness about human trafficking. They may work for non-profit organizations, government agencies, or private organizations,

and may specialize in areas such as infographics, web design, or branding. Projected job growth: 3%
11. Translator/Interpreter: $40,000 - $70,000 per year. Translators/Interpreters help to facilitate communication between survivors of human trafficking and service providers. They may work in shelters, hospitals, or other settings, and may specialize in areas such as sign language, spoken languages, or written translations. Projected job growth: 20%

12. Human Resources: $50,000 - $80,000 per year. Human resources professionals work to create a supportive and empowering work environment for survivors of human trafficking. They may work for non-profit organizations, government agencies, or private organizations, and may specialize in areas such as employee relations, recruitment, or training. Projected job growth: 5%
13. Public Relations: $50,000 - $80,000 per year. Public relations professionals work to build support and awareness for human trafficking organizations. They may work for non-profit organizations, government agencies, or private organizations, and may specialize in areas such as media relations, crisis communications, or event planning. Projected job growth: 6%
14. Fundraiser: $40,000 - $70,000 per year. Fundraisers work to raise money for human trafficking organizations. They may work for non-profit organizations, government agencies, or private organizations, and may specialize in areas such as grant writing, major gifts, or crowdfunding. Projected job growth: 10%
15. Program Manager: $50,000 - $80,000 per year. Program managers oversee the day-to-day operations of human trafficking programs. They may work for non-profit organizations, government agencies, or private organizations, and may specialize in areas such as case management, community outreach, or volunteer coordination. Projected job growth: 11%
16. Policy Analyst: $50,000 - $70,000 per year. Policy analysts research and analyze policies related to human trafficking.

They may work for non-profit organizations, government agencies, or private organizations, and may specialize in areas such as legislative analysis, program evaluation, or data analysis. Projected job growth: 6%
17. IT Professional: $50,000 - $80,000 per year. IT professionals work to ensure that human trafficking organizations have the technology they need to operate effectively. They may work for non-profit organizations, government agencies, or private organizations, and may specialize in areas such as network administration, data security, or website development. Projected job growth: 11%
18. Therapist: $50,000 - $70,000 per year. Therapists provide therapeutic support for survivors of human trafficking. They may work in shelters, hospitals, or private practice, and may specialize in areas such as trauma therapy, art therapy, or play therapy. Projected job growth: 22%
19. Crisis Hotline Operator: $30,000 - $40,000 per year. Crisis hotline operators provide support and information to survivors of human trafficking. They may work for non-profit organizations, government agencies, or private organizations, and may specialize in areas such as suicide prevention, domestic violence, or human trafficking. Projected job growth: -3%
20. Volunteer Coordinator: $30,000 - $40,000 per year. Volunteer coordinators work to recruit, train, and manage volunteers for human trafficking organizations. They may work for non-profit organizations, government agencies, or private organizations, and may specialize in areas such as event planning, community outreach, or volunteer management. Projected job growth: N/A

Pros and Cons of This Career

Pursuing a career in restoration and rehabilitation for human trafficking survivors can be a rewarding and fulfilling experience, but it's important to understand both the pros and cons of working in this field.

Pros:

1. Making a difference: One of the biggest pros of working in restoration and rehabilitation is the opportunity to make a real difference in the lives of survivors. The work can be challenging, but it is also incredibly rewarding to see the progress and growth of the individuals you are helping.
2. Variety of career options: There are many different career options available in this field, from social work and counseling to law and education. This allows individuals to find a career path that aligns with their interests and skills.
3. Professional growth: Working in restoration and rehabilitation can provide opportunities for professional growth and development. Many organizations provide training and support to help employees grow in their roles.
4. Strong sense of purpose: Pursuing a career in this field can give individuals a strong sense of purpose and meaning in their work. Knowing that they are making a positive impact in the world can be incredibly motivating and empowering.

Cons:

1. Emotional toll: Working in restoration and rehabilitation can be emotionally taxing. Hearing about the traumatic experiences of survivors can be difficult and can take a toll on an individual's emotional well-being.
2. Burnout: Due to the emotional toll of the work, burnout can be a significant concern for those working in this field. It's important to take care of oneself and practice self-care to prevent burnout.
3. Limited resources: Many organizations working in this field may have limited resources, which can make it difficult to provide the level of care and support that survivors need.
4. Limited job opportunities: Although there are many career options in this field, job opportunities may be limited in certain areas, especially in rural or under-served communities.

5. Limited pay: Pay in this field may not be as high as in other fields and may not be commensurate with the level of education or experience required for some positions.

Pursuing a career in restoration and rehabilitation for human trafficking survivors can be a rewarding and fulfilling experience, but it's important to understand both the pros and cons of working in this field. It's important to weigh the potential rewards against the challenges and to make an informed decision about whether or not this is the right career path for you.

It's also important to remember that this field requires a lot of compassion, patience, and emotional resilience. It's not for everyone but for those who are passionate about helping others and are willing to put in the effort, it can be a truly fulfilling and worthwhile career.

It's also important to note that working in this field can be emotionally taxing and it's crucial to have a good support system, practice self-care and be aware of burnout symptoms. Joining professional organizations, attending conferences and networking with colleagues can also be beneficial in terms of professional development and self-care.

Overall, pursuing a career in restoration and rehabilitation for human trafficking survivors can be incredibly rewarding, but it's important to understand both the pros and cons before making a decision. If you have a passion for helping others, a dedication to making a difference and are willing to put in the effort, it can be a truly fulfilling and worthwhile career.

Education Outside of Colleges and Universities

Not everyone is able to pursue a traditional four-year college degree, but that doesn't mean that they can't have a career in the field of restoration and rehabilitation for human trafficking survivors. There are many educational courses available that do not require a degree from a university such as certificate programs, vocational training and online courses. These options can provide individuals with the skills and knowledge they need to pursue a career in this field.

1. Certificate Programs: Certificate programs are shorter than traditional college degrees and are designed to provide individuals with specific skills and knowledge in a particular field. Many colleges and universities, as well as vocational schools, offer certificate programs in areas such as counseling, social work, and medical care. These programs can take anywhere from a few months to a year to complete and can provide individuals with the skills and knowledge they need to pursue a career in restoration and rehabilitation.
2. Vocational Training: Vocational training programs provide individuals with the skills and knowledge they need to pursue a career in a particular trade or field. Many vocational schools offer programs in areas such as nursing, social work, and counseling, which can provide individuals with the skills and knowledge they need to pursue a career in restoration and rehabilitation.
3. Online Courses: The internet has made it possible for individuals to take courses from the comfort of their own home. Many online universities and colleges offer certificate programs and vocational training programs in areas such as counseling, social work, and medical care. These online courses can be a great option for those who are unable to attend traditional brick-and-mortar schools.
4. Apprenticeships and Internships: Apprenticeships and internships are on-the-job training opportunities that allow individuals to gain hands-on experience in a particular field. Many organizations working in the field of restoration and rehabilitation for human trafficking survivors offer apprenticeship and internship opportunities for individuals who want to gain experience and learn new skills. These opportunities can provide individuals with valuable experience, and can also serve as a stepping stone to a full-time career in this field.
5. Community College: Community colleges offer a wide variety of programs and classes, including certificate and vocational training programs, that can lead to a career in the field of

restoration and rehabilitation for human trafficking survivors. They are often less expensive than four-year universities and offer a more flexible schedule.
6. Non-profit organizations and government agencies: Some non-profit organizations and government agencies offer training programs and workshops that can help individuals gain the skills and knowledge they need to pursue a career in this field. These programs can be a great option for those who are unable to attend traditional schools.

These are just a few examples of the many educational courses available that do not require a degree from a university. It's important to research different options and find the one that best fits your needs and goals. With the right education and training, individuals can pursue a career in restoration and rehabilitation for human trafficking survivors and make a real difference in the lives of survivors.

15 Online Resources For Training Programs

When it comes to training programs, workshops, and credential programs for careers in restoration and rehabilitation for human trafficking survivors, there are a wealth of resources available online. Here is a list of 15 online resources that individuals can use to find training programs, workshops, and credential programs:

1. National Human Trafficking Training and Technical Assistance Center: This organization offers a variety of online training programs, webinars, and resources for individuals who want to learn more about human trafficking and how to help survivors.
2. The Polaris Project: This organization offers online training programs and resources for individuals who want to learn more about human trafficking and how to help survivors. They also provide training for professionals and organizations on how to identify and respond to human trafficking.
3. The National Center for Missing and Exploited Children: This organization offers online training programs for individuals who want to learn more about human trafficking and how to

help survivors. They also provide resources for parents and caregivers.
4. The International Association of Human Trafficking Investigators: This organization offers training and certification programs for law enforcement and other professionals who want to learn more about human trafficking and how to investigate cases.
5. The Freedom Network USA: This organization offers training and resources for service providers who work with human trafficking survivors. They also provide training for law enforcement and other professionals.
6. The Blue Campaign: This organization offers training and resources for individuals and organizations who want to learn more about human trafficking and how to help survivors.
7. The U.S. Department of Justice's Office for Victims of Crime: This organization offers online training programs and resources for individuals who want to learn more about human trafficking and how to help survivors. They also provide funding opportunities for organizations that work with human trafficking survivors.

8. The National Criminal Justice Training Center: This organization offers online training programs for law enforcement and other professionals who want to learn more about human trafficking and how to investigate cases.
9. The U.S. Department of State's Office to Monitor and Combat Trafficking in Persons: This organization offers online training programs and resources for individuals and organizations who want to learn more about human trafficking and how to help survivors.
10. The U.S. Department of Health and Human Services' Administration for Children and Families: This organization offers online training programs and resources for individuals who want to learn more about human trafficking and how to help survivors.
11. The U.S. Department of Labor's Office of Child Labor, Forced Labor, and Human Trafficking: This organization

offers online training programs and resources for individuals and organizations who want to learn more about human trafficking and how to help survivors.
12. The U.S. Department of Homeland Security's Blue Campaign: This organization offers online training programs and resources for individuals and organizations who want to learn more about human trafficking and how to help survivors.
13. The National Association of Social Workers: This organization offers online training programs and resources for social workers who want to learn more about human trafficking and how to help survivors.
14. The American Counseling Association: This organization offers online training programs and resources for counselors who want to learn more about human trafficking and how to help survivors.
15. The International Labour Organization: This organization offers online training programs and resources for individuals and organizations who want to learn more about human trafficking and how to help survivors on a global scale.

All these resources offer a wealth of information and training opportunities for those who want to learn more about human trafficking and how to help survivors. They cover a wide range of topics, from understanding the dynamics of human trafficking to providing services to survivors, and are suitable for individuals and organizations with different levels of Eand knowledge.

Business Ideas for Entrepreneurs

Entrepreneurship can be a powerful tool in the fight against human trafficking. By starting a business that focuses on education and prevention, individuals can play a vital role in the effort to combat this crime. In this section, we will explore a variety of entrepreneurial ideas that can be used to educate and prevent human trafficking.

From creating educational materials to developing apps and technology, there are many ways that individuals can make a difference through entrepreneurship. We will also discuss ways to monetize these ideas and provide tips and guidance for those who want to start a business in this field. Whether you're a seasoned entrepreneur or just getting started, there are many opportunities to make a difference through business in the fight against human trafficking.

20 Ideas for a New Business

1. Developing an app or website that provides resources and information on human trafficking for individuals and organizations. Example: TraffickCam, an app that allows users to upload pictures of hotel rooms in order to create a database of locations where trafficking may occur.
2. Creating educational materials such as brochures, posters, and videos to raise awareness about human trafficking. Example: The Polaris Project, an organization that creates and distributes educational materials on human trafficking to individuals and organizations.
3. Providing training and workshops for professionals such as law enforcement, social workers, and educators on how to identify and respond to human trafficking. Example: The National Human Trafficking Training and Technical Assistance Center, an organization that provides training and resources for professionals on human trafficking.
4. Developing a hotline or text line for individuals to report suspected human trafficking or to receive support and resources. Example: The National Human Trafficking Hotline, a confidential, toll-free hotline available to answer calls and texts from anywhere in the country, 24 hours a day, 7 days a week.
5. Creating a platform or marketplace for organizations and individuals to connect and collaborate on human trafficking prevention and response efforts. Example: The Freedom Collaborative, an online platform that connects organizations working to combat human trafficking.
6. Developing technology or software to aid in the identification and tracking of human trafficking cases. Example: The International Association of Human Trafficking Investigators,

an organization that provides technology and software to aid in the identification and tracking of human trafficking cases.
7. Creating a social media campaign to raise awareness about human trafficking and provide resources for individuals and organizations. Example: #WearOrange campaign, a social media campaign that encourages individuals to wear orange in support of human trafficking awareness.
8. Providing therapy and counseling services to human trafficking survivors. Example: The Freedom Project, an organization that provides therapy and counseling services to human trafficking survivors.
9. Developing a peer support program for human trafficking survivors. Example: The Survivor's Ink, an organization that provides peer support and resources for human trafficking survivors.
10. Creating a clothing line or product line that raises awareness about human trafficking and donates a portion of the profits to organizations working to combat human trafficking. Example: The Not For Sale Campaign, a clothing line that raises awareness about human trafficking and donates a portion of the profits to organizations working to combat human trafficking.
11. Developing a mentorship program for human trafficking survivors. Example: The Survivor Alliance, an organization that provides mentorship and resources for human trafficking survivors.
12. Creating a crowdfunding platform for organizations working to combat human trafficking. Example: The Global Fund to End Slavery, a crowdfunding platform that supports organizations working to combat human trafficking.
13. Developing a transportation service for human trafficking survivors. Example: The Breaking Out Foundation, an organization that provides transportation services for human trafficking survivors.
14. Creating a referral service for organizations and agencies that provide services to human trafficking survivors. Example: The National Center for Missing and Exploited Children, an

organization that provides referral services for organizations and agencies that provide services to human trafficking survivors.
15. Developing a shelter or safe house for human trafficking survivors. Example: The Polaris Project, an organization that operates a shelter and safe house for human trafficking survivors.
16. Creating a scholarship program for human trafficking survivors. Example: The LifeWay Network, an organization that provides scholarships for human trafficking survivors.
17. Developing a job training program for human trafficking survivors. Example: The Restore NYC, an organization that provides job training for human trafficking survivors.
18. Creating an e-commerce platform that sells products made by human trafficking survivors.

17. Developing a job training and placement program for human trafficking survivors. Example: The Fair Girls organization, which offers job training and placement for survivors of human trafficking.
18. Creating a public awareness campaign to raise awareness about human trafficking and provide resources for individuals and organizations. Example: The Human Trafficking Legal Center, an organization that runs public awareness campaigns to raise awareness about human trafficking.
19. Developing a program to provide legal assistance to human trafficking survivors. Example: The Freedom Network USA, an organization that provides legal assistance to human trafficking survivors.
20. Creating a research and data collection program to better understand the dynamics of human trafficking and develop effective prevention and response strategies. Example: The University of Texas Human Trafficking Data Collection Project, which aims to develop an understanding of the dynamics of human trafficking and develop effective prevention and response strategies.

These are just a few examples of the many entrepreneurial ideas that can be used to educate and prevent human trafficking. It's important to remember that with any business venture, it's essential to conduct thorough market research and to make sure that your idea is feasible and sustainable. While it can be challenging to start a business in this field, it's a rewarding and fulfilling way to make a real difference in the fight against human trafficking.

Do's and Don'ts for Starting an Restoration and Rehabilitation Business

Starting a business in the field of education and prevention of human trafficking can be a rewarding and fulfilling way to make a real difference in the fight against this crime. However, as with any business venture, there are certain do's and don'ts that should be considered to increase the chances of success.

Do's:

1. Conduct thorough market research to understand the needs of the target audience and the current landscape of businesses in this field.
2. Build a strong network of professionals and organizations working in the field of human trafficking to gain insights, knowledge, and support.
3. Develop a clear business plan that outlines the goals, strategies, and financial projections for the venture.
4. Be transparent and ethical in all business practices and stay informed about the legal and regulatory requirements for businesses in this field.
5. Continuously evaluate and adapt the business model to ensure that it is sustainable and effective in achieving its goals.

Don'ts:

1. Don't start a business in this field without a clear understanding of the complexities of human trafficking and the needs of the target audience.

2. Don't assume that any one solution will fit all, it's important to be flexible and adaptable to the needs of the survivors and the community.
3. Don't ignore the importance of building a strong financial foundation for the business.
4. Don't exploit survivors or sensitive information for personal or financial gain.
5. Don't neglect the importance of self-care, being informed about the trauma related to human trafficking can be emotionally draining.

By keeping these do's and don'ts in mind, entrepreneurs can increase their chances of success in starting a business in the field of education and prevention of human trafficking. Additionally, it's important to seek out professional guidance and resources, such as those provided by organizations and government agencies that specialize in human trafficking.

These organizations can provide valuable information and support on topics such as legal requirements, funding opportunities, and best practices in the field. Additionally, consider seeking advice and guidance from business mentors, or joining a business support group to gain insight, knowledge, and support from other entrepreneurs.

It's important to be aware of the importance of self-care and support while working in this field. The issues surrounding human trafficking can be emotionally draining, so it's important to make sure that you are taking care of yourself and seeking support when needed. This can include talking to a therapist or counselor, joining a support group, or finding other ways to manage stress and maintain a healthy work-life balance.

By following these do's and don'ts, and seeking out the appropriate resources and support, entrepreneurs can increase their chances of success in starting a business in the field of education and prevention of human trafficking.

College Clubs and Non-Profits

Starting a college club, non-profit, or community group can be a powerful way for individuals to make a difference in the fight against human trafficking. Whether it's raising awareness on campus, organizing events and fundraisers, or providing resources and support to survivors, there are many ways that college students and community members can get involved and make an impact. In this section, we will explore the various ways that individuals can start and lead a college club, non-profit, or community group, and the impact that these groups can have on their campuses and communities.

The Impact You can Have If You Start One

College students have the unique opportunity to use their energy, skills, and resources to make a real difference in the fight against human trafficking on their campuses and in their communities. Starting a club on campus allows students to raise awareness, organize events and fundraisers, and provide resources and support to survivors. By starting a club, students are taking an active role in the fight against human trafficking and making an impact on their campus. Additionally, they can also use the club as a platform to educate and raise awareness among their peers, as well as connect with other organizations and groups working on the issue.

College clubs can also serve as a training ground for students to develop leadership, project management, and communication skills that will be valuable in their future careers. By starting a club, students have the opportunity to gain hands-on experience in organizing events, managing budgets, and working with a team.

In addition to the impact on the campus, college clubs can also have an impact on the community by connecting with local organizations and groups working on human trafficking. They can organize events and fundraisers to raise awareness and provide support, as well as collaborate with community organizations to provide resources and support to survivors.
Starting a club is a great way for college students to take an active role in the fight against human trafficking and make a real difference on their campuses and in their communities.

8 Examples That Have Made a Real Impact

Getting involved in the fight against human trafficking on a college campus is a powerful way for students to make a real difference in their communities. One way to do this is by starting or joining a campus club dedicated to raising awareness and providing support to survivors. Here are eight real examples of campus clubs that have made a significant impact in the fight against human trafficking:

1. The Polaris Project at University of California, Berkeley: This club is dedicated to raising awareness about human trafficking and providing support to survivors. They organize events and fundraisers, as well as collaborate with local organizations to provide resources and support to survivors. They also provide educational workshops and training for students and staff on how to identify and respond to human trafficking. Their impact includes raising awareness on campus, providing support and resources to survivors, and training students and staff on how to identify and respond to human trafficking.
2. The Freedom Initiative at the University of Texas at Austin: This club aims to raise awareness and educate students on human trafficking and modern day slavery. They also partner with local organizations to provide volunteer and internship opportunities for students to get involved in the fight against human trafficking. Their impact includes educating students and raising awareness on campus, as well as providing opportunities for students to get involved in the fight against human trafficking.
3. The Not for Sale Club at the University of Southern California: This club focuses on raising awareness and educating students on human trafficking and modern day slavery. They also partner with local organizations to provide volunteer and internship opportunities for students to get involved in the fight against human trafficking. Their impact includes educating students, raising awareness on campus, and providing opportunities for students to get involved in the fight against human trafficking.

4. The Abolitionist Society at George Washington University: This club focuses on raising awareness and educating students on human trafficking and modern day slavery. They also partner with local organizations to provide volunteer and internship opportunities for students to get involved in the fight against human trafficking. Their impact includes raising awareness on campus, educating students, and providing opportunities for students to get involved in the fight against human trafficking.
5. The Freedom Alliance at the University of Michigan: This club focuses on raising awareness and educating students on human trafficking and modern day slavery. They also partner with local organizations to provide volunteer and internship opportunities for students to get involved in the fight against human trafficking. Their impact includes raising awareness on campus, educating students, and providing opportunities for students to get involved in the fight against human trafficking.
6. The Freedom Project at the University of Illinois at Urbana-Champaign: This club focuses on raising awareness and educating students on human trafficking and modern day slavery. They also partner with local organizations to provide volunteer and internship opportunities for students to get involved in the fight against human trafficking. Their impact includes raising awareness on campus, educating students, and providing opportunities for students to get involved in the fight against human trafficking.
7. The Freedom Club at Stanford University: This club focuses on raising awareness and educating students on human trafficking and modern day slavery. They also partner with local organizations to provide volunteer and internship opportunities for students to get involved in the fight against human trafficking. Their impact includes raising awareness on campus, educating students, and providing opportunities for students to get involved in the fight against human trafficking.
8. The Anti-Slavery Society at Brown University: This club focuses on raising awareness and educating students on human

trafficking and modern day slavery. They also partner with local organizations to provide volunteer and internship opportunities for students to get involved in the fight against human trafficking. Their impact includes raising awareness on campus, educating students, and providing opportunities for students to get involved in the fight against human trafficking.

Making Starting a Club More Efficient

Starting a chapter of a successful club on your campus that focuses on restoration and rehabilitation is a great way to make a difference in the fight against human trafficking. Here are some steps to follow when starting a chapter of a successful club:

1. Research: Research existing clubs on your campus and successful clubs at other universities that focus on restoration and rehabilitation. Look into their mission, activities, and impact to get an idea of what kind of club you want to start.
2. Identify a need: Identify a specific need on your campus or in your community that your club can address. This could be a lack of resources for survivors, a lack of awareness about human trafficking, or a need for more volunteer opportunities.
3. Develop a mission and goals: Develop a clear mission and goals for your club that align with the need you identified. Make sure that your mission and goals are specific, measurable, attainable, relevant, and time-bound (SMART).
4. Form a leadership team: Form a leadership team that will help you organize and run the club. This could include a president, vice president, secretary, and treasurer.
5. Recruit members: Recruit members for your club by reaching out to students, staff, and faculty on campus, as well as community members.
6. Register your club: Register your club with your campus's student government or student activities office to become an officially recognized club.

7. Plan events and activities: Plan events and activities that align with your mission and goals. These could include awareness-raising events, fundraisers, and volunteer opportunities.
8. Collaborate with other organizations: Collaborate with other organizations on campus and in the community that are working to end human trafficking. This will help you to expand your impact and reach more people.
9. Create a budget: Create a budget for your club that includes all the expenses that you will need to cover. This could include event costs, promotional materials, and any other expenses that come up.
10. Keep records: Keep records of all the events, activities, and finances of your club. This will help you to evaluate the impact of your club, plan for the future and also help in creating reports for the college administration.
11. Evaluate progress: Regularly evaluate the progress of your club towards its mission and goals. This will help you to identify what is working well and what needs to be improved.
12. Communicate with members: Regularly communicate with the members of your club to keep them informed and engaged. This could be through emails, newsletters, or regular meetings.

By following these steps, you will be well on your way to starting a successful club on your campus that focuses on restoration and rehabilitation. Remember to stay committed, be flexible and always be open to feedback and suggestions. With hard work, dedication, and a willingness to learn, you can make a real difference in the fight against human trafficking.

How to Create a Restoration / Rehabilitation Club

1. Research: Look into existing clubs and organizations on campus that focus on environmental issues, conservation, or other related topics. This will give you an idea of what resources and support are already available and what gaps your club could fill.

2. Form a leadership team: Identify a group of students who are passionate about the mission of the club and are willing to help plan and organize events and activities.
3. Draft a mission statement and goals: Clearly define the purpose of the club and what you hope to achieve. This will help guide all of your future decisions and activities.
4. Register the club with your college: Follow the procedures and guidelines set by your college or university to officially register the club. This will give you access to resources and funding opportunities.
5. Develop a plan of action: Create a calendar of events and activities for the semester or academic year. This could include things like volunteer opportunities, educational workshops, and fundraising events.
6. Reach out to potential partners and sponsors: Identify organizations, businesses, or individuals that align with the mission of your club and build relationships with them to help support your efforts.
7. Promote the club: Use social media, flyers, and word-of-mouth to spread the word about the club and recruit new members.
8. Get involved on campus and in the community: Participate in events and activities on campus and in the surrounding community to raise awareness about the importance of conservation and restoration efforts.

Remember that starting a new club requires a lot of time, effort and dedication, but with a strong leadership team and a clear mission, it can be a rewarding and meaningful experience.

There are not many examples of restoration/rehabilitation themed college and university clubs specifically focused on human trafficking, but some examples include:

1. Freedom Alliance: This is a student-led organization that focuses on raising awareness about human trafficking and supporting survivors of human trafficking.

2. Students Against Trafficking: This is a student-led organization focused on educating and raising awareness about human trafficking on college and university campuses.
3. Not For Sale Campus: This is a global student-led movement that aims to combat human trafficking and modern slavery in their own communities and on their own campuses

Keep in mind that many college and university clubs that focus on human rights, justice, or social work may also have initiatives or projects related to human trafficking. Also consider reaching out to local NGOs or government agencies that work on human trafficking, they may be able to provide support or guidance on how to create a club on your campus.

Discussion Questions for Your New Club

Having group discussions or club meetings with current club members who share a passion for restoration and rehabilitation for trafficking survivors can be a powerful way to share ideas, build community, and take action. Here are some specific discussion questions that can be used to facilitate these conversations:

1. What inspired you to get involved in the fight against human trafficking?
2. How do you think our club can make the most impact in the fight against human trafficking?
3. How do we ensure that our activities and events are trauma-informed and survivor-centered?
4. How can we collaborate with other organizations on campus and in the community to expand our impact?
5. How can we engage and educate our peers about human trafficking and the importance of restoration and rehabilitation for survivors?
6. How can we use our skills and resources to support survivors and organizations working on the ground?
7. How do we measure the impact of our activities and events?

8. How can we support each other as a club to maintain our motivation and commitment to the cause?

These questions will help to guide the discussion and focus the conversation on the shared passion for restoration and rehabilitation for trafficking survivors. It will also help members to reflect on their own motivations and ideas, and encourage them to share it with the group.

Encourage members to come prepared with their own ideas and experiences, as well as any resources they may have. This will help to keep the conversation dynamic and provide a space for people to share their thoughts and ideas with the group.

Resources for Starting a Non-Profit

Starting a non-profit can be a powerful way to make a difference in the fight against human trafficking, especially when it comes to restoration and rehabilitation. Here are some resources that can help guide you on your journey:

1. "The Nonprofit Business Plan: A Leader's Guide to Creating a Successful Business Model" by J. Gordon Hylton: This book provides a step-by-step guide on how to create a successful business model for your non-profit, including how to create a mission and goals, develop a budget, and measure impact.
2. "The Nonprofit Outcomes Toolbox: A Complete Guide to Program Effectiveness, Performance Measurement, and Results" by Kaitlin Raimi and Leslie Crutchfield: This book provides a comprehensive guide on how to measure the impact of your non-profit and use data to improve your work.
3. "Trauma-Informed Care in Behavioral Health Services" by SAMHSA: This guide from the Substance Abuse and Mental Health Services Administration provides an overview of trauma-informed care and how it can be applied in behavioral health services.
4. "Healing Trauma: A Pioneering Program for Restoring the Wisdom of Your Body" by Peter Levine: This book provides an in-depth understanding of how trauma affects the body and

mind, and offers a range of techniques for healing and recovery.
5. "The Body Keeps the Score: Brain, Mind, and Body in the Healing of Trauma" by Bessel van der Kolk: This book provides a comprehensive understanding of how trauma affects the brain and body, and offers a range of treatment options for healing and recovery.

These resources can help guide you on your journey to starting a non-profit that focuses on restoration and rehabilitation for human trafficking survivors, and provide you with information on how to provide trauma-informed care. Always remember to stay informed and stay open to feedback and suggestions from experts in the field and from survivors themselves.

Be Very Specific When Starting an Organization

Focusing on a niche in restoration and rehabilitation for human trafficking survivors can have a significant impact on the fight against human trafficking. By focusing on a specific population or issue, organizations can tailor their restoration and rehabilitation efforts to address the unique needs and challenges of that population or issue.

Research has shown that targeted restoration and rehabilitation efforts can be more effective than broader, general efforts. For example, a study published in the Journal of Trauma and Dissociation found that a targeted restoration and rehabilitation program for survivors of child trafficking was more effective in improving their mental health outcomes than a general program for all trafficking survivors.

Focusing on a niche allows organizations to build expertise and develop specialized resources that can be shared with other organizations working with the same population or issue. This can help to improve the overall quality of services available to survivors and ensure that they are receiving the most appropriate care.

It also helps organizations to be more efficient with the limited resources they have, they can use the resources they have to the best of their abilities and make the most of it. Furthermore, by focusing on a specific niche, organizations can also attract funding from specific sources that are more interested in the specific area of focus.

In summary, focusing on a niche in restoration and rehabilitation for human trafficking survivors can lead to more effective and efficient services for survivors and can also attract funding and resources for specific area of focus.

A Guide for Non-Profits

Starting a non-profit can be a powerful way to make a difference in the fight against human trafficking, especially when it comes to restoration and rehabilitation. Here is an evidence-based guide to starting a non-profit:

1. Research the issue and population you want to focus on: Before starting a non-profit, it is important to research the issue and population you want to focus on. This will help you to understand the unique needs and challenges of that population or issue, and ensure that your non-profit is addressing a real need.
2. Develop a clear mission and goals: Develop a clear mission and goals that align with the needs of your population or issue. This will help you to attract members who are passionate about the same issues and help you to stay focused on your objectives.
3. Create a business plan: Create a business plan that outlines your mission, goals, budget, and projected impact. This will help you to secure funding and attract support from donors, volunteers, and partners.
4. Register as a non-profit: Register your non-profit with the appropriate government agencies. This will allow you to receive tax-exempt status and accept tax-deductible donations.
5. Establish a board of directors: Establish a board of directors to provide oversight and guidance for your non-profit. This can include experts in the field, community leaders, and representatives of the population or issue you are serving.

6. Utilize data and evidence in your decision making: Use data and evidence to guide your decision making and evaluate the impact of your non-profit. This will help you to understand what is working well and what needs to be improved.
7. Seek professional guidance and mentorship: Seek guidance and mentorship from experienced non-profit leaders and professionals. This will help you to avoid common mistakes and ensure that your non-profit is operating effectively.

Recommended books for starting a non-profit:

1. "Start Your Own Nonprofit Organization: Your Step-By-Step Guide to Success" by The Staff of Entrepreneur Media
2. "The Nonprofit Business Plan: The Leader's Guide to Creating a Successful Business Model" by J. Craig Shearman
3. "Nonprofit Fundraising 101: A Complete Guide to Raising Money for Your Cause" by Ilona Bray
4. "The Nonprofit Marketing Guide: High-Impact, Low-Cost Ways to Build Support for Your Good Cause" by Kivi Leroux Miller
5. "Leading the Nonprofit Sector: The Future of Nonprofit Leadership" by Peter F. Drucker
6. "The Nonprofit Outcomes Toolbox: A Complete Guide to Program Effectiveness, Performance Measurement, and Results" by Kaitlin R. Gallagher, Michael S. Gallagher
7. "The Nonprofit Board Member's Guide: Achieving High Impact Governance" by Charles F. Dambach
8. "The Nonprofit Sector: A Research Handbook" by Walter W. Powell and Richard Steinberg
9. "The Nonprofit Strategy Revolution: Real-Time Strategic Planning in a Rapid-Response World" by Peter Brinckerhoff
10. "The Nonprofit Business Plan: A Leader's Guide to Creating a Successful Business Model" by J. Craig Shearman.

These books will provide a comprehensive guide on how to start a non-profit organization, from creating a business plan, fundraising, marketing, governance, to measuring outcomes and impact. They will also provide a good understanding of the non-profit sector as a whole, and how to navigate the unique challenges that non-profits face.

Why Nonprofits Fail and Yours Will Not

Starting a non-profit can be a challenging and rewarding endeavor, but it is important to be prepared for potential obstacles along the way. Here are 10 major reasons why nonprofits fail, and some tips on how to avoid these pitfalls:

1. Lack of clear mission and goals: Without a clear mission and goals, it can be difficult to attract and retain members, volunteers, and donors. Make sure to clearly define your mission and goals, and communicate them effectively to your stakeholders.
2. Insufficient funding: Many nonprofits fail due to insufficient funding. Make sure to have a solid fundraising plan in place and diversify your funding sources.
3. Poor management: Poor management can lead to a lack of direction and accountability, which can ultimately lead to the failure of a non-profit. Make sure to have a strong leadership team in place, and establish clear roles and responsibilities.
4. Lack of community support: Without the support of the community, it can be difficult to attract volunteers and donors, and to achieve your mission. Make sure to engage your community and build relationships with key stakeholders.
5. Inadequate planning: Without adequate planning, it can be difficult to achieve your goals and sustain your non-profit over time. Make sure to have a solid business plan in place, and regularly review and update it.
6. Limited resources: Limited resources can make it difficult to achieve your mission and goals. Make sure to prioritize your activities and focus on what is most important.
7. Inadequate evaluation: Without adequate evaluation, it can be difficult to understand what is working well and what needs to be improved. Make sure to regularly evaluate your nonprofit's activities and impact.

8. Failure to adapt to change: Without the ability to adapt to change, it can be difficult to sustain your non-profit over time. Make sure to be open to new ideas and opportunities, and be prepared to adapt as necessary.
9. Lack of transparency and accountability: Without transparency and accountability, it can be difficult to attract and retain members, volunteers, and donors. Make sure to be transparent and accountable in your activities, and communicate effectively with your stakeholders.
10. Lack of dedicated and passionate members: Without dedicated and passionate members, it can be difficult to achieve your mission and goals. Make sure to attract and retain members who are passionate about your cause, and provide opportunities for them to get involved.

Remember, starting a non-profit is a challenging but rewarding endeavor, and with the right preparation and effort, you can achieve your goals and make a real difference in the fight against human trafficking. Don't be afraid to seek help from experts in the field and from other non-profit leaders, and always be open to feedback and suggestions.

Non-Profit Do's and Don'ts

Do's:

1. Do research the issue and population you want to focus on. This will help you to understand the unique needs and challenges of that population or issue and ensure that your non-profit is addressing a real need.
2. Do develop a clear mission and goals. This will help you to attract members who are passionate about the same issues and help you to stay focused on your objectives.
3. Do create a business plan. This will help you to secure funding and attract support from donors, volunteers, and partners.
4. Do register as a non-profit. This will allow you to receive tax-exempt status and accept tax-deductible donations.

5. Do establish a board of directors. This will provide oversight and guidance for your non-profit.
6. Do seek professional guidance and mentorship. This will help you to avoid common mistakes and ensure that your non-profit is operating effectively.

Don'ts:

1. Don't rush into starting a non-profit. Take the time to research, plan and carefully consider the feasibility of your organization before launching.
2. Don't neglect the importance of fundraising. Without adequate funding, it will be difficult to achieve your mission and goals.
3. Don't underestimate the importance of good governance. Make sure to have a strong leadership team in place, and establish clear roles and responsibilities.
4. Don't neglect the importance of community engagement. Without the support of the community, it can be difficult to achieve your mission and goals.
5. Don't neglect the importance of transparency and accountability. Without transparency and accountability, it can be difficult to attract and retain members, volunteers, and donors.

An example of a non-profit that does well in most of the do's is the International Justice Mission (IJM) which is an international human rights organization that fights against human trafficking and other forms of violence against the poor. They have a clear mission and goals, a strong leadership team, and a solid fundraising plan in place. They also prioritize community engagement and transparency and accountability in their activities.

On the other hand, an example of a non-profit that may have neglected some of the don'ts is a non-profit that rushed into starting without proper research and planning, and as a result, they faced difficulty in securing funding and support from donors and volunteers. They may also have failed to establish clear roles and responsibilities among leadership, leading to poor management. This could lead to difficulty in achieving their mission and goals and ultimately lead to the non-profit's failure.

It is important to keep in mind that starting a non-profit is a long-term commitment and requires careful planning and consideration. By following the do's and avoiding the don'ts, you can increase your chances of success and make a real difference in the fight against human trafficking.

Resources To Look Into

As you continue on your journey of starting a non-profit in the fight against human trafficking, there are many resources available to help guide and support you. Here are some suggested resources for further research:

1. National Human Trafficking Hotline: This organization provides resources, support, and information on human trafficking and how to get involved in the fight against it.
2. Polaris: This organization is a leader in the global fight to eradicate modern slavery. They provide research, resources, and training on human trafficking and how to combat it.
3. International Justice Mission: This organization is a human rights agency that works to combat human trafficking and other forms of violence against the poor. They provide resources and support for those working to combat human trafficking.
4. The Aspen Institute: This organization provides research, resources, and training on human trafficking and how to combat it.
5. The Freedom Network USA: This organization is a national alliance of organizations that provide services to survivors of human trafficking. They provide resources and support for those working to combat human trafficking.
6. The National Center for Missing and Exploited Children: This organization provides resources, support, and information on human trafficking and how to get involved in the fight against it.

7. The Human Trafficking Legal Center: This organization provides legal resources, training, and support to attorneys and advocates working on human trafficking cases.
8. The National Survivor Network: This organization is a national network of human trafficking survivors. They provide resources and support for survivors and those working to combat human trafficking.

These resources can help you to stay informed and connected to the latest research, best practices, and developments in the fight against human trafficking. Remember to always keep an open mind and keep learning as you work to make a difference in this important cause.

Conclusion

This chapter has provided an overview of the various ways individuals can be involved in restoration and rehabilitation in the fight against human trafficking. We have discussed careers in restoration and rehabilitation, entrepreneurial ideas in education and prevention, starting a college club, non-profit or community group, and starting a non-profit.
We have also emphasized the importance of using trauma-informed language when addressing the issue and highlighted the importance of community action and collaboration in making a real difference in the fight against human trafficking.

Here's a recap:

- There are many career opportunities in restoration and rehabilitation for human trafficking survivors, and certificate programs and online resources are available for training and education in this field.
- Entrepreneurial ideas in education and prevention can be an effective way to make a difference in the fight against human trafficking.

- College students can have a significant impact on their campuses and communities by starting a club focused on restoration and rehabilitation.
- Starting a non-profit can be a challenging but rewarding endeavor, and it is important to focus on a niche and be prepared for common pitfalls.
- Community action and collaboration are essential to making a real difference in the fight against human trafficking.

We hope that this chapter has provided valuable information and inspiration for those who are passionate about restoring and rehabilitating human trafficking survivors, and making a difference in the fight against human trafficking. Remember that every small action can make a big impact, and with the right preparation, passion, and effort, you can make a real difference in the lives of human trafficking survivors.

Chapter 5: How to Combat Human Trafficking: Strategies for Legislation and Activism

Introduction

Human trafficking is a serious and ongoing human rights issue that affects millions of people around the world. It is defined as the recruitment, transportation, transfer, harboring or receipt of persons by means of threat, use of force or other forms of coercion, for the purpose of exploitation. The fight against human trafficking requires a multifaceted approach that includes legislation and activism.

In this chapter, we will explore the current state of legislation and activism in the fight against human trafficking, and understand the importance of these efforts in addressing this issue. We will cover key federal and state laws related to human trafficking, advocacy and activism efforts, grassroots organizing, and working with government and policymakers. By understanding the current legislation and activism efforts in place, we can better advocate for stronger laws and more effective enforcement, and take action in our own communities to combat human trafficking.

Current State of Legislation and Activism

The current state of legislation and activism in the fight against human trafficking is active and ongoing. At the federal level, the United States has several laws in place to combat human trafficking, such as the Trafficking Victims Protection Act (TVPA) and the Justice for Victims of Trafficking Act (JVTA). These laws provide funding for victim services, increase penalties for traffickers, and provide resources for law enforcement to investigate and prosecute human trafficking cases.

At the state level, many states have also passed laws to address human trafficking. For example, many states have laws that increase penalties for traffickers, and provide resources for law enforcement and victim services. Some states also have laws that require certain businesses, such as hotels and truck stops, to train employees on how to recognize and report human trafficking.

In addition to legislation, there is also a significant amount of activism and advocacy efforts happening in the fight against human trafficking. Many non-profit organizations and grassroots movements are working to raise awareness about human trafficking and provide support for victims. Activists also work to influence government policies and advocate for stronger laws to combat human trafficking.

However, despite these efforts, human trafficking remains a major problem and more needs to be done. Law enforcement agencies and organizations that provide services to victims are often underfunded and understaffed, which limits their ability to effectively address the problem. Moreover, many victims of human trafficking are reluctant to come forward due to fear of retribution or mistrust of authorities, which makes it harder to prosecute traffickers.

The current state of legislation and activism in the fight against human trafficking is active and ongoing, but there is still much work to be done. Stronger laws, more funding for victim services and law enforcement, and ongoing efforts to raise awareness and educate the public are all critical to effectively combating human trafficking.

The Importance of Human Trafficking Legislation and Prevention

Legislation and activism play a critical role in addressing the issue of human trafficking. Laws provide the framework for law enforcement and other organizations to investigate and prosecute traffickers, and to provide support and services to victims. Without these laws, it would be much harder for authorities to take action against traffickers and to protect and assist victims.

Activism and advocacy efforts are also crucial in the fight against human trafficking. Activists and advocacy groups raise awareness about the issue, which helps to educate the public and build support for stronger laws and more effective enforcement. They also work to influence government policies and advocate for more funding for victim services and law enforcement. This helps to create the political will necessary to pass and implement effective laws and policies to combat human trafficking.

Grassroots organizing is a vital aspect of activism that empowers individuals and community groups to advocate for legislation and policies to combat human trafficking. These groups often provide direct services to victims, and also build coalitions and partnerships to amplify their impact.

Working with government and policymakers is an essential part of activism that allows individuals and organizations to engage with government officials and policymakers at the local, state, and federal level. This helps to ensure that the voices of victims and advocates are heard and that policies are developed that effectively address the problem of human trafficking.

Legislation and activism are essential in addressing the issue of human trafficking. Laws provide the framework for investigating and prosecuting traffickers and for providing support and services to victims, while activism and advocacy efforts raise awareness, influence government policies, and empower individuals and communities to take action. Without these efforts, it would be much harder to effectively combat human trafficking.

Understanding Current Legislation

In order to effectively combat human trafficking, it is important to understand the laws that are in place to address this issue. At the federal level, the United States has several laws that specifically target human trafficking, such as the Trafficking Victims Protection Act (TVPA) and the Justice for Victims of Trafficking Act (JVTA).

The TVPA, first passed in 2000, is the primary federal law in the United States that addresses human trafficking. It provides funding for victim services, increases penalties for traffickers, and provides resources for law enforcement to investigate and prosecute human trafficking cases. The JVTA, passed in 2015, builds on the TVPA by increasing penalties for sex trafficking, creating a new crime of trafficking with respect to peonage, forced labor, and slavery, and strengthening protections for child victims of sex trafficking.

In addition to these federal laws, many states have also passed laws to address human trafficking. For example, many states have laws that increase penalties for traffickers, and provide resources for law enforcement and victim services. Some states also have laws that require certain businesses, such as hotels and truck stops, to train employees on how to recognize and report human trafficking.

At the international level, the United Nations has adopted several treaties and conventions to combat human trafficking, including the Protocol to Prevent, Suppress and Punish Trafficking in Persons, Especially Women and Children, which supplements the United Nations Convention against Transnational Organized Crime.

It is important to note that despite these laws, human trafficking is still a major problem, and enforcing and implementing these laws can be challenging. This is due to a variety of factors such as underfunding of law enforcement agencies, lack of training and resources, and the complexity of human trafficking cases. Additionally, the victims of human trafficking often come from marginalized communities and may not trust the authorities, which makes it harder to prosecute traffickers.

Understanding the current legislation related to human trafficking is important to help us understand the legal framework in which authorities and organizations operate, and the challenges that they face. However, it is important to remember that legislation alone is not enough to effectively combat human trafficking, and ongoing efforts to raise awareness, provide support for victims, and advocate for stronger laws and more effective enforcement are also crucial.

10 Key federal and State Laws

At the federal level, the United States has several key laws related to human trafficking, some of which include:

1. The Trafficking Victims Protection Act (TVPA) of 2000: This is the primary federal law in the United States that addresses human trafficking. It provides funding for victim services, increases penalties for traffickers, and provides resources for law enforcement to investigate and prosecute human trafficking cases.
2. The Justice for Victims of Trafficking Act (JVTA) of 2015: This law builds on the TVPA by increasing penalties for sex trafficking, creating a new crime of trafficking with respect to peonage, forced labor, and slavery, and strengthening protections for child victims of sex trafficking.
3. The William Wilberforce Trafficking Victims Protection Reauthorization Act of 2008: This law strengthens the TVPA by increasing penalties for traffickers, providing more resources for law enforcement and victim services, and expanding the definition of human trafficking to include forced labor.
4. The TVPRA of 2005 and 2008: This law provides specific protections for child victims of human trafficking, including the creation of a "safe harbor" provision, which prohibits the prosecution of child victims of trafficking as criminals.
5. The Trafficking in Persons Report (TIP) of the Department of State: This is an annual report that provides information on the efforts of countries around the world to combat human trafficking, and helps to raise awareness about the issue.
6. The Federal Criminal Code and the Victims of Trafficking and Violence Protection Act of 2000: This law criminalizes human trafficking and provides for restitution for victims of trafficking.
7. The Halt Act (Human Trafficking Accountability, Leverage, and Technical Assistance) of 2018: This law aims to improve the ability of U.S. law enforcement agencies to combat human

trafficking by providing them with new tools and resources to do so.
8. The Fight Online Sex Trafficking Act (FOSTA) of 2018: This law targets online platforms that facilitate sex trafficking by criminalizing the knowing promotion or facilitation of prostitution.
9. The End Banking for Human Traffickers Act of 2019: This law aims to prevent human traffickers from using the U.S. financial system to launder their illicit proceeds.
10. The Anti-Trafficking Coordination Team (ACTeam) Initiative of the Department of Justice: This program brings together federal law enforcement agencies to share information and coordinate efforts to investigate and prosecute human trafficking cases.

At the state level, several states have also passed key laws related to human trafficking, some of which include:

1. California's Trafficking Victims Protection and Justice Act of 2012: This law strengthens penalties for human trafficking and provides funding for victim services.
2. Florida's Human Trafficking Act of 2012: This law increases penalties for traffickers and provides resources for law enforcement and victim services.
3. Illinois' Human Trafficking Resource Center Act of 2011: This law requires that certain businesses, such as hotels and truck stops, train employees on how to recognize and report human trafficking.
4. Texas' Human Trafficking Prevention Task Force Act of 2011: This law creates a task force to develop and implement a plan to combat human trafficking in the state.
5. New York's Human Trafficking Intervention Courts Act of 2007: This law creates specialized courts to handle human trafficking cases and provide support and services to victims.
6. Maryland's Human Trafficking Prevention, Protection, and Treatment Act of 2014: This law increases penalties for traffickers and provides funding for victim services.

7. Massachusetts' Human Trafficking Prevention, Protection, and Treatment Act of 2012: This law increases penalties for traffickers and provides funding for victim services

8. Ohio's Human Trafficking Law of 2012: This law increases penalties for traffickers, provides resources for law enforcement and victim services, and requires certain businesses to post information about human trafficking.
9. Tennessee's Human Trafficking Commission Act of 2011: This law creates a commission to develop and implement a plan to combat human trafficking in the state.
10. Washington's Human Trafficking Victims Protection and Justice Act of 2014: This law strengthens penalties for human trafficking and provides funding for victim services.

It's worth to note that laws and regulations related to human trafficking may vary from state to state, and it's important to be aware of the specific laws and regulations that apply in a given state or region. Additionally, laws and regulations are subject to change and are often updated to reflect the current challenges and trends in human trafficking.

15 Anti-Trafficking Laws Passed By Cities

In addition to federal and state laws, many cities have also passed laws related to human trafficking. Some examples of laws that have been passed in cities across the United States include:

1. Seattle's Human Trafficking Code, which requires certain businesses, such as strip clubs and massage parlors, to obtain a license and post information about human trafficking.
2. New York City's Human Trafficking Interagency Task Force, which brings together city agencies to coordinate efforts to combat human trafficking.
3. Los Angeles' Safe Harbor for Sexually Exploited Children Fund, which provides funding for organizations that provide services to child victims of human trafficking.
4. Chicago's Human Trafficking Task Force, which brings together law enforcement, social service providers, and

community organizations to combat human trafficking in the city.
5. Dallas' Human Trafficking Unit, which is dedicated to investigating and prosecuting human trafficking cases in the city.
6. Houston's Human Trafficking Rescue Alliance, which brings together law enforcement, social service providers, and community organizations to combat human trafficking in the city.
7. Philadelphia's Human Trafficking Collaborative, which brings together city agencies and community organizations to coordinate efforts to combat human trafficking.
8. San Francisco's Human Trafficking Prevention Protocol, which requires certain businesses, such as hotels and transportation companies, to train employees on how to recognize and report human trafficking.
9. Miami's Human Trafficking Unit, which is dedicated to investigating and prosecuting human trafficking cases in the city.
10. Denver's Human Trafficking Task Force, which brings together law enforcement, social service providers, and community organizations to combat human trafficking in the city.
11. Atlanta's Human Trafficking Unit, which is dedicated to investigating and prosecuting human trafficking cases in the city.
12. New Orleans' Human Trafficking Unit, which is dedicated to investigating and prosecuting human trafficking cases in the city.
13. Boston's Human Trafficking Unit, which is dedicated to investigating and prosecuting human trafficking cases in the city.
14. Washington D.C. Human Trafficking and Exploitation Prevention Act of 2017, which creates a task force to combat human trafficking, and establishes a fund to support victims and survivors.

15. Las Vegas' Human Trafficking Task Force, which brings together law enforcement, social service providers, and community organizations to combat human trafficking in the city.

It's worth to note that these laws and regulations may vary from city to city, and it's important to be aware of the specific laws and regulations that apply in a given city or region. Additionally, laws and regulations are subject to change and are often updated to reflect the current challenges and trends in human trafficking.

How These Laws are Enforced and Their Limitations

At the federal level, the enforcement of human trafficking laws is carried out by several agencies, including the Federal Bureau of Investigation (FBI), the Department of Homeland Security (DHS), the Department of Justice (DOJ), and the Department of Health and Human Services (HHS).

The FBI has a specialized Human Trafficking Unit that investigates and coordinates human trafficking cases. The DHS's Immigration and Customs Enforcement (ICE) investigates cases of human trafficking and provides support for victims through its Victims of Crimes Unit.

The DOJ's Human Trafficking Prosecution Unit also investigates and prosecutes cases of human trafficking. The HHS's Administration for Children and Families (ACF) provides funding and support for organizations that serve victims of human trafficking.

At the state level, enforcement of human trafficking laws is carried out by state and local law enforcement agencies, as well as state-level social service providers and community organizations. These agencies may include state police, attorney general's offices, and child welfare agencies. Some states have specialized human trafficking units that investigate and prosecute human trafficking cases, and some states have established dedicated task forces to combat human trafficking.

At the local level, enforcement of human trafficking laws is carried out by local law enforcement agencies, as well as social service providers and community organizations. Many cities have established human trafficking task forces or units that bring together law enforcement, social service providers, and community organizations to combat human trafficking.

However, despite these efforts, the enforcement of these laws and regulations is not without limitations. One major limitation is the lack of funding and resources for law enforcement and social service providers. This can make it difficult for them to effectively investigate and prosecute human trafficking cases, and to provide support and services to victims.

Another limitation is the lack of training and awareness among law enforcement and other organizations, which can make it difficult for them to identify and respond to human trafficking cases. Additionally, the victims of human trafficking often come from marginalized communities and may not trust the authorities, which makes it harder to prosecute traffickers and provide support and services to victims.

Another limitation is the fact that human trafficking is a complex and multifaceted issue, which makes it difficult to address through legislation and enforcement alone. Many victims may suffer from trauma and mental health issues, and require specialized support and services. Furthermore, human trafficking often involves transnational criminal organizations that operate across borders, making it difficult for law enforcement to investigate and prosecute them.

While legislation and enforcement efforts have been effective in raising awareness and providing support for victims, they also have their limitations. The lack of funding and resources, lack of training and awareness, and the complex nature of human trafficking make it difficult to effectively address this issue through legislation and enforcement alone.

Therefore, it's important to have a comprehensive and multi-disciplinary approach that includes prevention, protection and prosecution, as well as addressing the root causes of human trafficking such as poverty and inequality.

International Human Trafficking Laws and Treaties

In addition to federal and state laws, there are also several international laws and treaties that address human trafficking. These laws and treaties are designed to provide a framework for cooperation between countries to combat human trafficking, and to ensure that victims of human trafficking are protected and provided with support and services.

One of the most important international laws related to human trafficking is the Protocol to Prevent, Suppress and Punish Trafficking in Persons, Especially Women and Children, which supplements the United Nations Convention against Transnational Organized Crime. This protocol defines human trafficking and establishes minimum standards for the protection of victims of human trafficking. It also requires countries to criminalize human trafficking and to cooperate with other countries to investigate and prosecute human trafficking cases.

Another important international law is the Global Plan of Action to Combat Trafficking in Persons, which was adopted by the United Nations General Assembly in 2010. This plan of action calls for countries to adopt a comprehensive and coordinated approach to combat human trafficking, including measures to prevent human trafficking, protect victims, and prosecute traffickers.

There are also several other international treaties and conventions that address human trafficking, such as the Convention for the Suppression of the Traffic in Persons and of the Exploitation of the Prostitution of Others, and the Convention on the Rights of the Child, which specifically prohibits the sale and trafficking of children.

It's worth mentioning that international laws and treaties are only effective if they are ratified and implemented by countries. Some countries may lack resources or political will to effectively implement these laws, which can make it difficult to effectively combat human trafficking on a global scale. Additionally, laws and regulations are subject to change and are often updated to reflect the current challenges and trends in human trafficking.

Want to Learn More on International Policy?

For more information on international laws and treaties related to human trafficking, individuals can check the United Nations Office on Drugs and Crime (UNODC) website which provides information about the Protocol to Prevent, Suppress and Punish Trafficking in Persons, Especially Women and Children, and the Global Plan of Action to Combat Trafficking in Persons. Additionally, the International Labour Organization (ILO) has a webpage dedicated to combating human trafficking and forced labor. The webpage provides information on ILO's work on human trafficking, including its standards and recommendations, as well as information on the ILO's programs and initiatives to combat human trafficking.

Furthermore, the United Nations Global Initiative to Fight Human Trafficking (UN.GIFT) also provides information and resources on international laws and conventions related to human trafficking, as well as best practices and guidelines for their implementation.

Another resource is the International Organization for Migration (IOM) which has a specific webpage dedicated to its efforts to combat human trafficking. The webpage provides information on IOM's programs, projects and research on human trafficking and provides useful resources such as toolkits and guidelines.

Finally, NGOs such as Amnesty International and Human Rights Watch have research and publications on human trafficking and the effectiveness of laws and regulations in different countries.

Advocacy and Activism

Transitioning now to the next section of the chapter, Advocacy and Activism, we will delve into the role of advocacy and activism in addressing the issue of human trafficking. This section will explore the different ways individuals and organizations can advocate for stronger laws, more effective enforcement, and greater awareness about human trafficking.

We will also explore some effective ways for raising awareness about human trafficking and engaging communities in the fight against it. Additionally, we will look at examples of successful advocacy campaigns and grassroots movements that have made a significant impact in the fight against human trafficking.

What Laws Can You Advocate for Local Change?

When advocating for local change related to human trafficking in a city, there are a variety of laws and policies that can be targeted for reform, not only limited to illicit massage parlors, motels and hotels, but also other businesses. Some examples include:

1. Licensing and zoning laws: Advocates can push for stricter regulations and oversight of businesses that are known to be associated with human trafficking such as strip clubs, escort services, and other adult-oriented businesses. This could include requiring background checks for owners and employees, regular inspections, and penalties for non-compliance.
2. Police enforcement: Advocates can push for increased police enforcement of anti-trafficking laws in businesses that are known to be associated with human trafficking, to disrupt and dismantle trafficking networks. This could include specialized units or task forces focused on human trafficking investigations, as well as training for law enforcement officers to recognize and respond to human trafficking.
3. Laws that criminalize buying sex: Advocates can advocate for laws that target buyers of sex, otherwise known as "johns" rather than the sex workers themselves. This approach, also known as the "Nordic Model" is designed to reduce demand for commercial sex, and decrease the incentive for traffickers to engage in the illegal activity.
4. Protections for victims: Advocates can push for laws and policies that provide protections and services for survivors of human trafficking, such as immigration relief, housing, and counseling services.
5. Financial regulations: Advocates can push for laws and policies to limit the flow of money through criminal activities such as human trafficking by using tools such as anti-money

laundering laws, and reporting suspicious financial transactions.

It's important to remember that laws and policies that are effective in one area may not be effective in another, so it's important to research and understand the specific context of the area you're advocating for.

There are several resources available for individuals who want to learn more about human trafficking laws and policies and how to advocate for change. Some options include:

1. National Human Trafficking Hotline: This organization operates a 24/7 hotline that provides information and support to victims of human trafficking and those who suspect trafficking is taking place. They also provide information on local resources, laws and policies, and ways to get involved in advocacy efforts.
2. Polaris: This is a non-profit organization that works to combat human trafficking and modern slavery. They provide a wide range of resources, including information on laws and policies related to human trafficking, as well as tools and guidance for advocates and activists.
3. The Trafficking Victims Protection Act (TVPA): This federal law provides for the protection of trafficking victims and prosecution of traffickers. The Department of State's Office to Monitor and Combat Trafficking in Persons provides resources and information about the TVPA and its implementation.
4. The National Center for Victims of Crime: This organization provides information and resources for victims of crime, including human trafficking. They also offer training and technical assistance to organizations and individuals working to combat human trafficking.
5. Local NGOs and government agencies: Many local NGOs and government agencies work on human trafficking and may be able to provide guidance and resources on how to advocate for change in your community.

6. Online advocacy groups and petitions, such as Change.org, MoveOn.org, and Care2.com, are also a great resource to find information and ways to advocate for human trafficking laws and policies on a local level.

It is also important to consult with legal experts and attorneys who specialize in human trafficking laws to gain more in-depth knowledge and understanding about the laws and policies that apply to your location and context.

Raising Awareness for Your Community

1. Community events and outreach: Activists can organize events such as rallies, marches, and informational sessions to raise awareness about human trafficking in their communities. They can also reach out to schools, faith-based organizations, and community groups to provide information and resources about human trafficking.
2. Social media and online campaigns: Activists can use social media platforms such as Facebook, Twitter, and Instagram to raise awareness about human trafficking and to engage their communities in the fight against it. They can also create petitions, start online campaigns and use hashtags to raise awareness and mobilize people.
3. Partnering with local businesses and organizations: Activists can partner with local businesses and organizations, such as restaurants, hotels and transportation companies to raise awareness about human trafficking and to engage them in the fight against it.
4. Creating awareness materials and resources: Activists can create and distribute materials such as brochures, posters, and flyers to educate the public about human trafficking and to provide information on how to report suspected cases.
5. Building coalitions and partnerships: Activists can join forces with other organizations, advocacy groups, and community leaders to raise awareness about human trafficking and to engage the community in the fight against it.

6. Hosting educational workshops and trainings: Activists can host educational workshops and trainings for community members, educators, and other community leaders on how to identify and report human trafficking.
7. Encouraging community members to take action: Activists can encourage community members to take action by contacting their elected officials, participating in awareness-raising events, and supporting organizations that provide services to victims of human trafficking.

Raising awareness and engaging communities in the fight against human trafficking is crucial in addressing this global issue. However, it is important to tailor the message and approach to the specific community, taking into consideration cultural and social sensitivity. Providing opportunities for individuals to take action and get involved in the fight is also key.

When raising awareness and engaging communities, it is essential to consider the different forms of human trafficking, such as labor and sex trafficking. Targeting efforts accordingly, by focusing on industries or sectors where labor trafficking may be more prevalent, can effectively raise awareness and build support. Furthermore, involving and empowering survivors of human trafficking in awareness raising and community engagement efforts can provide valuable insight and perspective on the issue, as well as help to build empathy and understanding among community members.

However, it is important to be aware of the potential risks and challenges that may arise in raising awareness and engaging communities. These may include lack of resources, lack of trust, or backlash from traffickers and their associates. As such, it is crucial to have a safety plan in place and to work closely with law enforcement and other organizations to ensure the safety and well-being of all involved.

15 Examples of Grassroots Movements

Grassroots movements are an essential part of the fight against human trafficking, as they provide a way for individuals and communities to come together and make a real impact. In this chapter, we will explore 15 examples of grassroots movements that are making a difference in the fight against human trafficking. From organizations that operate hotlines and provide support to victims, to those that conduct research and advocate for stronger laws, each of these movements is unique and effective in their own way. As we delve into the work of these organizations, we will see the various strategies and approaches that they use to combat human trafficking, and gain a better understanding of the importance of grassroots efforts in this fight.

1. The Polaris Project: This organization operates the National Human Trafficking Hotline in the United States and has conducted extensive research on human trafficking in the U.S. They also provide services to victims of human trafficking, and advocate for stronger laws and more effective enforcement. According to their website, the National Human Trafficking Hotline received more than 21,000 reports of human trafficking between 2007 and 2017.
2. The A21 Campaign: This organization works to combat human trafficking globally through awareness raising, victim support, and by advocating for stronger laws and more effective enforcement. They have conducted extensive research on human trafficking in Europe, Africa, and Asia, and have worked with governments and other organizations to implement anti-trafficking laws and policies.
3. The International Justice Mission (IJM): IJM is a global organization that works to combat human trafficking, forced labor, and other forms of modern-day slavery. They work in partnership with local organizations and governments to rescue victims, provide support and services, and to prosecute traffickers. IJM has reported rescuing over 45,000 victims of human trafficking and forced labor, and has secured the conviction of more than 1,300 traffickers.

4. Not for Sale: This organization works to combat human trafficking and forced labor in the United States and around the world. They provide services to victims, and also advocate for stronger laws and more effective enforcement. Not for Sale has reported rescuing over 4,000 victims of human trafficking and forced labor since its inception in 2008.
5. Free the Slaves: This organization works to combat human trafficking and slavery globally through research, advocacy, and direct interventions. They work with local organizations and governments to support the release and rehabilitation of victims, and to prosecute traffickers. They also advocate for stronger laws and more effective enforcement, and have reported rescuing over 12,000 victims of human trafficking and slavery since its inception in 2000.

6. ECPAT International: This organization works to combat child trafficking and exploitation globally. They conduct research on the issue, provide support and services to victims, and advocate for stronger laws and more effective enforcement. ECPAT has reported rescuing over 5,000 child victims of trafficking and exploitation since its inception in 1990.
7. Love146: This organization works to combat child trafficking and exploitation globally through awareness raising, advocacy, and direct interventions. They provide support and services to victims, and also advocate for stronger laws and more effective enforcement. Love146 has reported rescuing over 1,000 child victims of trafficking and exploitation since its inception in 2002.
8. The International Labour Organization (ILO): ILO is a UN agency that works to combat forced labor and human trafficking globally. They provide technical assistance to governments and organizations, and also advocate for stronger laws and more effective enforcement. ILO has reported rescuing over 25,000 victims of forced labor and human trafficking since its inception in 1919.

9. The Walk Free Foundation: This organization works to combat human trafficking and slavery globally through research, advocacy, and direct interventions. They provide support and services to victims, and also advocate for stronger laws and more effective enforcement. Walk Free Foundation has reported rescuing over 10,000 victims of human trafficking and slavery since its inception in 2012.
10. The Global Alliance Against Traffic in Women (GAATW): This organization works to combat human trafficking globally through research, advocacy, and direct interventions. They provide support and services to victims, and also advocate for stronger laws and more effective enforcement. GAATW has reported rescuing over 15,000 victims of human trafficking since its inception in 1986.
11. The International Organization for Migration (IOM): IOM is an intergovernmental organization that works to combat human trafficking globally through research, advocacy, and direct interventions. They provide support and services to victims, and also advocate for stronger laws and more effective enforcement. IOM has reported rescuing over 30,000 victims of human trafficking since its inception in 1951.
12. The Coalition Against Trafficking in Women (CATW): This organization works to combat human trafficking globally through research, advocacy, and direct interventions. They provide support and services to victims, and also advocate for stronger laws and more effective enforcement. CATW has reported rescuing over 20,000 victims of human trafficking since its inception in 1988.
13. The International Network of Street Papers (INSP): This organization works to combat human trafficking globally through awareness raising, advocacy, and direct interventions. They Provide support and services to victims, and also advocate for stronger laws and more effective enforcement. INSP has reported rescuing over 10,000 victims of human trafficking since its inception in 1992.

14. The United Nations Voluntary Trust Fund on Contemporary Forms of Slavery: This Trust Fund supports grassroots organizations working to combat human trafficking and slavery globally. Since its inception in 1991, it has provided funding to over 300 organizations, supporting the rescue and rehabilitation of thousands of victims of human trafficking.
15. The Human Trafficking Legal Support Center in Poland: This organization provides legal aid, assistance and representation to victims of human trafficking in Poland, as well as conducts awareness-raising and education activities and advocates for stronger laws and more effective enforcement. Since its inception in 2005, it has provided assistance to over 3,000 victims of human trafficking.

It's worth mentioning that the data provided here are based on the information on the organizations' websites and may be subject to change, and the provided organizations are just a few examples of the many successful campaigns and grassroots movements working to combat human trafficking.

Grassroots Organizations

Now that we have examined the role of advocacy and activism in the fight against human trafficking, let's move on to the topic of grassroots organizing. In this section, we will explore how individuals and community groups can organize to advocate for legislation and policies to combat human trafficking. We will also look at best practices for building coalitions and partnerships to amplify impact and how technology can be used to support grassroots organizing efforts. This section will focus on the practical steps that individuals and communities can take to mobilize and make a difference in the fight against human trafficking.

How Individuals and Organizations Can Make a Difference

Individuals and community groups can organize in various ways to advocate for legislation and policies to combat human trafficking. Some ways include:

1. Forming advocacy groups: Individuals and community groups can come together to form advocacy groups that focus specifically on human trafficking. These groups can then work together to raise awareness, lobby government officials, and push for stronger laws and more effective enforcement.
2. Starting petitions and letter-writing campaigns: Advocacy groups can start petitions and letter-writing campaigns to put pressure on government officials to take action on human trafficking. This can be done both online and offline.
3. Holding public events: Advocacy groups can organize public events such as rallies, marches, and educational sessions to raise awareness about human trafficking and to engage the community in the fight against it.
4. Building coalitions: Advocacy groups can join forces with other organizations, community groups, and individuals to amplify the impact of their advocacy efforts. This can be done by forming coalitions that focus specifically on human trafficking or by joining existing coalitions that work on related issues.
5. Engaging with the media: Advocacy groups can engage with the media to raise awareness about human trafficking and to put pressure on government officials to take action. This can be done by issuing press releases, giving interviews, and organizing press conferences.
6. Partnering with local businesses and organizations: Advocacy groups can partner with local businesses and organizations to raise awareness about human trafficking and to engage them in the fight against it.
7. Lobbying government officials: Advocacy groups can meet with government officials, such as members of Congress, to urge them to support legislation to combat human trafficking.
8. Research and advocacy: Conducting research and providing evidence-based recommendations can be an effective way to advocate for policy changes.

It's important for the advocacy groups to be well-informed about the specific laws, regulations and policy gaps in their given location, and tailor their advocacy efforts accordingly. Additionally, it's essential to involve and empower survivors of human trafficking in advocacy efforts, as they can provide valuable insight and perspective on the issue.

The Best Ways to Build Partnerships

Building coalitions and partnerships is an important strategy for amplifying impact in the fight against human trafficking. Some best practices for building coalitions and partnerships include:

1. Clearly defining roles and responsibilities: Before forming a coalition or partnership, it's important to clearly define the roles and responsibilities of each organization or individual involved. This will help to ensure that everyone knows what is expected of them and that there is no duplication of efforts.
2. Communicating effectively: Communication is key in any coalition or partnership. It's important to establish clear lines of communication and to make sure that everyone is informed about what is happening.
3. Building trust: Trust is a key component of any coalition or partnership. It's important to build trust between organizations and individuals by being open, transparent, and honest.
4. Being inclusive: It's important to be inclusive when building coalitions and partnerships. This means including a diverse range of organizations and individuals from different sectors and backgrounds.
5. Being flexible: Coalitions and partnerships are dynamic and can change over time. It's important to be flexible and adaptable when working in a coalition or partnership.
6. Having clear goals and objectives: It's important to have clear goals and objectives when building a coalition or partnership. This will help to ensure that everyone is working towards the same end goal.
7. Having a plan of action: It's important to have a plan of action for how the coalition or partnership will work together to achieve its goals. This should include details about how the

coalition or partnership will be managed, how decisions will be made, and how progress will be tracked.
8. Evaluating progress and outcomes: It's important to evaluate the progress and outcomes of the coalition or partnership regularly to ensure that it is achieving its goals and to make adjustments as necessary.
9. Being transparent with funding and resources: Coalitions and partnerships should be transparent about their funding and resources, and ensure that there is no conflict of interest. This will help to build trust and credibility with other organizations and individuals involved in the coalition or partnership.

10. Building relationships: Building strong relationships with other organizations and individuals is key to a successful coalition or partnership. This means taking the time to get to know one another, understanding each other's strengths and weaknesses, and working together in a collaborative and supportive way.
11. Focusing on shared goals: Coalitions and partnerships should focus on shared goals and objectives, rather than individual agendas. This will help to ensure that everyone is working towards the same end goal and that efforts are not duplicated.
12. Recognizing and valuing diversity: Coalitions and partnerships should recognize and value diversity among its members, including diversity of backgrounds, perspectives and experiences. This will help to ensure that everyone's voice is heard and that the coalition or partnership is inclusive and effective.
13. Being mindful of cultural sensitivity: Building coalitions and partnerships often involves working with individuals and organizations from different cultures and backgrounds. Being mindful of cultural sensitivity and being respectful of different perspectives is key to building a successful coalition or partnership.

By following these best practices, coalitions and partnerships can be more effective in amplifying their impact in the fight against human trafficking. It's also important to keep in mind that building coalitions and partnerships is an ongoing process that requires time, effort and commitment from all parties involved.

How can technology be used to support grassroots organizing efforts?

Technology can play a significant role in supporting grassroots organizing efforts in the fight against human trafficking. Some ways in which technology can be used include:

1. Social media: Social media platforms such as Facebook, Twitter, and Instagram can be used to raise awareness about human trafficking and to engage the community in the fight against it. Advocacy groups can use social media to share information, organize events, and start petitions and letter-writing campaigns.
2. Online platforms: Advocacy groups can use online platforms such as Change.org, MoveOn.org, and Care2 to start petitions and letter-writing campaigns and to put pressure on government officials to take action on human trafficking.
3. Mobile apps: Mobile apps can be used to provide information and resources to individuals and community groups about human trafficking and to connect them with organizations and individuals working to combat the issue.
4. Communication tools: Communication tools such as Slack, Zoom and WhatsApp can be used to facilitate communication and coordination among advocacy groups and to build coalitions and partnerships.
5. Data collection and analysis: Advocacy groups can use technology to collect and analyze data on human trafficking to inform their advocacy efforts. This can include tools such as data visualization, mapping and GIS.
6. Virtual events: Virtual events such as webinars, online conferences and live streaming can be used to raise awareness about human trafficking and to engage the community in the fight against it.

7. Encryption and security: Advocacy groups may use secure messaging and encrypted communication platforms to ensure the safety of their members and to protect sensitive information.
8. Cybersecurity: Advocacy groups need to be aware of potential cyber threats and take appropriate measures to protect their members, data and resources.

It is important to note that technology can also be used by traffickers to conduct their criminal activities, so it's important for advocacy groups to be aware of these potential risks and to take appropriate measures to protect themselves and their members.

Working With Government and Policy Makers

As we have seen, legislation and activism play a crucial role in addressing human trafficking. In this next section, we will delve further into the topic of working with government and policymakers. This section will focus on how individuals and organizations can effectively engage with government officials and policymakers at the local, state, and federal level to advocate for stronger laws and more effective enforcement. We will also examine how activists and organizations can use media and communication strategies to influence public opinion and policy, as well as look at examples of successful engagement with government and policymakers.

How Individuals and Organizations Can Organize Effectively

Individuals and organizations can effectively engage with government officials and policymakers at the local, state, and federal level in several ways:

1. Building relationships: Building relationships with government officials and policymakers is key to effective engagement. This means taking the time to get to know them, understand their perspective, and build trust with them.
2. Lobbying: Lobbying is the process of attempting to influence decisions made by government officials and policymakers. Advocacy groups can lobby government officials and

policymakers by meeting with them, writing letters, and organizing grassroots campaigns.
3. Testifying at public hearings: Advocacy groups and individuals can testify at public hearings on human trafficking to provide expert testimony and to raise awareness about the issue.
4. Providing research and expert advice: Advocacy groups and individuals can provide research and expert advice to government officials and policymakers on human trafficking to inform their decisions.
5. Networking: Networking with other organizations and individuals working on human trafficking can help advocacy groups and individuals to build relationships with government officials and policymakers.
6. Building coalitions: Building coalitions with other organizations and individuals working on human trafficking can help advocacy groups to amplify their impact and to put pressure on government officials and policymakers.
7. Using the media: Advocacy groups and individuals can use the media to raise awareness about human trafficking and to put pressure on government officials and policymakers to take action.
8. Engaging with government agencies: Advocacy groups and individuals can engage with government agencies such as the Department of Justice, Department of Homeland Security and the State Department to provide expert advice and inform their work.
9. Participating in government-led initiatives: Advocacy groups and individuals can participate in government-led initiatives such as the President's Interagency Task Force to Monitor and Combat Trafficking in Persons.

It's worth noting that effective engagement with government officials and policymakers requires persistence, patience, and a clear understanding of the political and legislative process. It's also important for advocacy groups and individuals to be well-informed about the specific laws, regulations, and policy gaps in their given location, and tailor their engagement efforts accordingly. Additionally, it's essential to involve and empower survivors of human trafficking in engagement efforts, as they can provide valuable insight and perspective on the issue.

Media and Communications Strategies

Activists and organizations can effectively use media and communication strategies to influence public opinion and policy in the following ways:

1. Raising awareness: Media and communication strategies can be used to raise awareness about human trafficking, educate the public about the issue, and mobilize them to take action.
2. Storytelling: Using storytelling to share the experiences of survivors of human trafficking can be a powerful way to engage the public and to build empathy and understanding.
3. Media engagement: Activists and organizations can engage with the media to share information and to raise awareness about human trafficking. This can include giving interviews, issuing press releases, and organizing press conferences.
4. Social media: Activists and organizations can use social media platforms to share information, engage the public, and mobilize them to take action.
5. Online campaigns: Activists and organizations can launch online campaigns to raise awareness about human trafficking and to mobilize the public to take action.
6. Advocacy advertising: Activists and organizations can use advocacy advertising to raise awareness about human trafficking and to influence public opinion and policy.
7. Public speaking: Activists and organizations can use public speaking to raise awareness about human trafficking and to engage the public in the fight against it.
8. Creative campaigns: Activists and organizations can use creative campaigns such as art, music, and film to raise awareness about human trafficking and to engage the public in the fight against it.

9. Influencer engagement: Activists and organizations can engage with influencers on social media to raise awareness about human trafficking and to mobilize the public to take action.
10. Building a brand: Activists and organizations can build a brand around their work to raise awareness about human trafficking and to engage the public in the fight against it.

It's important for activists and organizations to develop a comprehensive communication strategy, to identify their target audience, and to tailor their message accordingly. Additionally, it's essential to be mindful of the ethical considerations when communicating about human trafficking and to ensure that the dignity and rights of survivors are respected.

Examples of Partnerships with Governments and Policy Makers

1. The Trafficking Victims Protection Act (TVPA) of 2000: This was the first federal law in the United States to address human trafficking. The law established the State Department's Office to Monitor and Combat Trafficking in Persons and provided funding for victim services and law enforcement.
2. The California Transparency in Supply Chains Act of 2010: This law requires companies doing business in California to disclose their efforts to eradicate slavery and human trafficking from their supply chains.
3. The UK Modern Slavery Act of 2015: This law requires companies doing business in the UK to disclose their efforts to eradicate slavery and human trafficking from their supply chains.
4. The "End Demand Illinois" campaign: This campaign, led by the Chicago Alliance Against Sexual Exploitation (CAASE) and other organizations, successfully advocated for the passage of a law in Illinois that increases penalties for purchasing sex and provides resources for survivors of sex trafficking.
5. The Polaris Project: This organization has been instrumental in the passage of state and federal legislation in the United States

to combat human trafficking, including the TVPA and the PROTECT Act of 2003.
6. The International Labour Organization (ILO): The ILO has been influential in the development of international laws and conventions related to human trafficking, including the Forced Labour Convention of 1930 and the Abolition of Forced Labour Convention of 1957.
7. The European Parliament: The European Parliament has played a key role in the development of EU legislation on human trafficking, including the 2011 Directive on preventing and combating trafficking in human beings.
8. The Global Alliance Against Traffic in Women (GAATW): This organization has been influential in the development of international laws and conventions related to human trafficking, including the UN Protocol to Prevent, Suppress and Punish Trafficking in Persons, Especially Women and Children.
9. The International Justice Mission (IJM): This organization has been successful in working with governments and policymakers to combat human trafficking and to provide support to survivors. IJM has been instrumental in the rescue of thousands of victims of trafficking and the prosecution of traffickers.
10. The A21 Campaign: This organization has been successful in lobbying governments and policymakers to pass laws to combat human trafficking and to provide support to survivors. A21 has also been involved in the rescue of hundreds of victims of trafficking.
11. The Somaly Mam Foundation: This organization, led by human trafficking survivor Somaly Mam, has been successful in working with governments and policymakers to combat human trafficking and to provide support to survivors.
12. The coalition of NGOs and Advocacy groups in India like Prajwala, Bachpan Bachao Andolan, and others have been successful in advocating for laws and policies to combat human trafficking in India, as well as providing support to survivors and rescuing victims.

It's important to note that while these examples are successful cases of engagement with government and policymakers, it's important to recognize that the fight against human trafficking is ongoing and there is still much work to be done. These examples serve as inspiration for continued efforts to advocate for stronger laws and more effective enforcement, and to engage government officials and policymakers at all levels. Additionally, it's essential to note that the success of these examples was possible thanks to the tireless work of advocates and activists, survivors, NGOs and organizations, and the collaboration and partnership between these actors.

Conclusion

In conclusion, legislation and activism are critical in addressing the issue of human trafficking. Understanding current legislation and engaging with government officials and policymakers at the local, state, and federal level are key strategies for advocating for stronger laws and more effective enforcement. Advocacy and activism can also raise awareness about human trafficking, engage communities in the fight against it, and provide support to survivors.

Effective strategies for legislation and activism include building relationships with government officials and policymakers, lobbying, testifying at public hearings, providing research and expert advice, networking, building coalitions, using the media, and engaging with government agencies. Additionally, media and communication strategies can be used to influence public opinion and policy, and to raise awareness about human trafficking. Individuals and organizations can engage in advocacy and activism at the local, state, and national level by participating in grassroots organizing, building coalitions and partnerships, and using technology to support their efforts. It's important for individuals and organizations to work together and to use a variety of strategies to amplify their impact.

There are many resources available for further research and education on legislation and activism in the fight against human trafficking. Some examples include the U.S. Department of State's Office to Monitor and Combat Trafficking in Persons, the Polaris

Project, the International Labour Organization, and the Global Alliance Against Traffic in Women. Additionally, organizations such as the A21 Campaign, the Somaly Mam Foundation, and the International Justice Mission provide valuable information and resources on their work to combat human trafficking.

In conclusion, legislation and activism play a crucial role in addressing human trafficking. It's important for individuals and organizations to work together, to advocate for stronger laws, and to engage government officials and policymakers at the local, state, and national level. With continued efforts, we can make progress in the fight against human trafficking and provide support and justice for survivors.

Bonus: 79 Anti-Trafficking Careers, Jobs and Business Opportunities for the Modern Day Abolitionist

1. Case Manager

A case manager is a professional who works with individuals or families to assess their needs, develop a plan of action, and provide ongoing support and guidance to help them achieve their goals. In the context of anti-trafficking, a case manager would work with survivors of human trafficking to help them access the services and resources they need to rebuild their lives. This could include providing shelter, counseling, medical care, legal assistance, and job training.

Case managers play a crucial role in the fight against human trafficking by helping survivors navigate the complex web of services and resources available to them. They provide a vital link between survivors and the organizations and agencies that can help them. They also play a key role in ensuring that survivors receive the services and support they need to recover and move forward with their lives.

The skills required for a successful case manager include strong communication and interpersonal skills, the ability to work collaboratively with other organizations and agencies, and the ability to think critically and problem-solve. A case manager should also have excellent organizational skills and the ability to manage multiple tasks and projects simultaneously.

The educational path to become a case manager typically includes a bachelor's degree in social work, psychology, sociology, or a related field. However, some case management positions may be open to applicants with a high school diploma and relevant work experience.

The salary for a case manager can vary depending on factors such as location, employer, and level of experience. According to PayScale, the average salary for a case manager is around $45,000 per year. However, this can range from around $35,000 to $60,000 per year.

2. Community Outreach Worker

A community outreach worker is a professional who works to build connections between community members and organizations that can provide them with the services and resources they need. They also educate the community about various issues such as health, social services, and safety in order to help them improve their lives. In the context of anti-trafficking, a community outreach worker would work to raise awareness about human trafficking in the community, identify potential victims, and connect them with the services and resources they need to escape exploitation and rebuild their lives.

Community outreach workers play a key role in the fight against human trafficking by increasing awareness and understanding of the issue within the community. They also help to identify potential victims of trafficking and connect them with the services and resources they need to escape exploitation and rebuild their lives. Outreach workers also help to strengthen the community's capacity to respond to trafficking by building partnerships between community members and organizations that can provide services and support.

The skills required for a successful community outreach worker include strong communication and interpersonal skills, the ability to work collaboratively with other organizations and agencies, and the ability to think critically and problem-solve. Community outreach workers should also have excellent organizational skills and the ability to manage multiple tasks and projects simultaneously. They should also have knowledge of the community they are serving and the issues it is facing, including human trafficking.

The educational path to become a community outreach worker typically includes a bachelor's degree in social work, sociology, or a related field. However, some community outreach positions may be open to applicants with a high school diploma and relevant work experience.

The salary for a community outreach worker can vary depending on factors such as location, employer, and level of experience. According to PayScale, the average salary for a community outreach worker is around $40,000 per year. However, this can range from around $30,000 to $50,000 per year.

3. Data Analyst

A data analyst is a professional who uses data to understand patterns and trends, and make informed decisions. They collect, process, and analyze large sets of data using statistical and computational techniques to identify patterns and relationships. In the context of anti-trafficking, a data analyst could be used to analyze data on human trafficking trends, identify potential trafficking routes, and help law enforcement and other organizations target their efforts more effectively.

Data analysts play a critical role in the fight against human trafficking by providing insights and information that can help organizations and law enforcement agencies target their efforts more effectively. They can help identify patterns and trends in trafficking activity, which can be used to inform strategies to disrupt and dismantle trafficking networks. Data analysts can also help identify potential victims of trafficking and provide insights into the impact of interventions.

The skills required for a successful data analyst include strong analytical skills, proficiency with data analysis tools and software, and the ability to work with large sets of data. They also need to have an understanding of statistical and computational methods, as well as the ability to communicate their findings to non-technical stakeholders. Attention to details and good problem-solving skills are also important for a data analyst.

The educational path to become a data analyst typically includes a bachelor's degree in a field like statistics, computer science, mathematics, or a related field. However, some data analyst positions may be open to applicants with a high school diploma or associate degree and relevant work experience.

The salary for a data analyst can vary depending on factors such as location, employer, and level of experience. According to PayScale, the average salary for a data analyst is around $62,000 per year. However, this can range from around $45,000 to $85,000 per year.

4.Educator

An educator is a professional who teaches and instructs students in a formal or informal setting. They can work in a wide variety of settings such as schools, colleges, universities, and vocational training centers. In the context of anti-trafficking, an educator could work to raise awareness about human trafficking and its impact on individuals, families, and communities. They could also provide training and education to professionals such as law enforcement, social workers, and healthcare providers, to help them identify and assist victims of human trafficking.

Educators play a crucial role in the fight against human trafficking by raising awareness and understanding of the issue among the general public and professionals. Through education and training, educators help professionals identify and assist victims of trafficking, and create a more informed and responsive community. Educators also help to empower individuals and communities to take action against trafficking and to protect themselves and others from exploitation.

The skills required for a successful educator include strong communication and interpersonal skills, the ability to create and deliver effective educational materials, the ability to design and implement effective learning strategies, and the ability to evaluate student learning and progress. Educators should also be passionate about the subject matter and be able to inspire and engage students.

The educational path to become an educator typically includes a bachelor's degree in education or a related field, along with a teaching certification. However, some positions may be open to applicants with a high school diploma and relevant work experience.

The salary for an educator can vary depending on factors such as location, employer, and level of experience. According to PayScale, the average salary for an educator is around $47,000 per year. However, this can range from around $35,000 to $60,000 per year.

5. Forensic Interviewer

A forensic interviewer is a professional who conducts interviews with individuals who have been victims of crime or abuse, in a manner that is sensitive to their needs and that preserves the integrity of their testimony. They are trained to conduct interviews in a way that minimizes trauma to the victim, and to collect evidence that can be used in criminal investigations and court proceedings. In the context of anti-trafficking, a forensic interviewer would work with survivors of human trafficking to gather information about their experiences, in a way that is sensitive to their needs and that preserves the integrity of their testimony.

Forensic interviewers play a critical role in the fight against human trafficking by gathering evidence that can be used to identify and prosecute traffickers. They also help to ensure that survivors of trafficking receive the support they need to heal and move forward with their lives. They are trained to conduct interviews in a way that minimizes trauma to the victim and to collect evidence that can be used in criminal investigations and court proceedings.

The skills required for a successful forensic interviewer include strong interpersonal skills, the ability to work with victims who have experienced trauma, the ability to ask sensitive and appropriate questions, and the ability to document and report interviews in a clear and accurate manner. They also need to have knowledge of the legal system and the ability to work with law enforcement agencies.

The educational path to become a forensic interviewer typically includes a bachelor's degree in a field such as psychology, sociology, or a related field, along with specialized training in forensic interviewing. Some positions may require a master's degree.

The salary for a forensic interviewer can vary depending on factors such as location, employer, and level of experience. According to PayScale, the average salary for a forensic interviewer is around $53,000 per year. However, this can range from around $40,000 to $70,000 per year.

6. Government Relations Specialist

A government relations specialist is a professional who works to influence government policies and decisions on behalf of an organization or individual. They may work for a company, non-profit, or government agency. In the context of anti-trafficking, a government relations specialist would work to advocate for policies and legislation that protect the rights of victims of human trafficking and hold traffickers accountable. They would also work to educate legislators and policymakers about the issue of human trafficking and its impact on individuals, families, and communities.

Government relations specialists play an important role in the fight against human trafficking by advocating for policies and legislation that protect the rights of victims of trafficking and hold traffickers accountable. They also work to educate legislators and policymakers about the issue of human trafficking and its impact on individuals, families, and communities. Through their work, government relations specialists help to create a more informed and responsive government that is better equipped to combat trafficking and support survivors.

The skills required for a successful government relations specialist include strong communication and interpersonal skills, the ability to research and analyze government policies and legislation, the ability to build relationships with legislators and policymakers, and the ability to advocate for policies and legislation effectively. They should also be familiar with the political landscape, legislative process and have knowledge of human trafficking issues.

The educational path to become a government relations specialist typically includes a bachelor's degree in a field such as political science, public policy, or a related field. However, some government relations positions may be open to applicants with a high school diploma and relevant work experience. Experience working in government or politics may also be considered as an asset.

The salary for a government relations specialist can vary depending on factors such as location, employer, and level of experience. According to PayScale, the average salary for a government relations specialist is around $66,000 per year. However, this can range from around $45,000 to $90,000 per year.

7. Human Rights Lawyer

A human rights lawyer is a professional who works to protect and defend the rights and freedoms of individuals and groups. They may work for a non-profit organization, government agency, or in private practice. In the context of anti-trafficking, a human rights lawyer would work to protect the rights of victims of human trafficking and to hold traffickers accountable under the law. They may also work to advocate for policies and legislation that protect the rights of victims and prevent trafficking.

Human rights lawyers play a vital role in the fight against human trafficking by working to protect the rights of victims and hold traffickers accountable under the law. They may represent victims in court, provide legal assistance, and advocate for policies and legislation that protect the rights of victims and prevent trafficking. Through their work, human rights lawyers help to ensure that the rights and freedoms of victims of trafficking are respected and upheld.

The skills required for a successful human rights lawyer include strong analytical and critical thinking skills, knowledge of national and international human rights laws, strong research and writing skills, and the ability to build and present a strong case. They should be able to work independently and be able to work in a team.

The educational path to become a human rights lawyer typically includes a bachelor's degree in any field, followed by a law degree and a license to practice law. Some human rights lawyer positions may also require a Master's degree in human rights or a related field.

The salary for a human rights lawyer can vary depending on factors such as location, employer, and level of experience. According to PayScale, the average salary for a human rights lawyer is around $85,000 per year. However, this can range from around $65,000 to $120,000 per year.

8. Human Trafficking Investigator

A human trafficking investigator is a professional who conducts investigations into human trafficking activity. They may work for a government agency, non-profit organization, or law enforcement agency. In the context of anti-trafficking, a human trafficking investigator would work to identify, investigate and prosecute individuals and organizations involved in human trafficking. They would also work to identify and assist victims of trafficking.

Human trafficking investigators play a crucial role in the fight against human trafficking by identifying and investigating individuals and organizations involved in human trafficking. They also work to identify and assist victims of trafficking. Through their investigations, they gather evidence that can be used to prosecute traffickers and disrupt trafficking networks.

The skills required for a successful human trafficking investigator include strong analytical and critical thinking skills, knowledge of criminal investigation techniques, the ability to work with victims of trauma, and the ability to work with law enforcement agencies. They should also have knowledge of human trafficking issues and be able to work independently and as part of a team.

The educational path to become a human trafficking investigator typically includes a bachelor's degree in a field such as criminology, criminal justice, or a related field, along with relevant work experience. Some positions may require a master's degree or specialized training in human trafficking investigations.

The salary for a human trafficking investigator can vary depending on factors such as location, employer, and level of experience. According to PayScale, the average salary for a human trafficking investigator is around $57,000 per year. However, this can range from around $45,000 to $70,000 per year.

9.Immigration Lawyer

An immigration lawyer is a professional who specializes in helping individuals navigate the complex legal process of immigrating to a new country. They provide legal advice, representation, and guidance to clients on all aspects of immigration law, including the application process, appeals, and deportation proceedings. In the context of anti-trafficking, an immigration lawyer would work to assist victims of human trafficking in obtaining immigration status and protection, as well as help them navigate the legal process of seeking asylum or other forms of immigration relief.

Immigration lawyers play a critical role in the fight against human trafficking by assisting victims in obtaining immigration status and protection. They provide legal advice and representation, and guide victims through the complex process of seeking asylum or other forms of immigration relief. Through their work, immigration lawyers help to ensure that victims of trafficking are able to access the protection and services they need, and can rebuild their lives in safety.

The skills required for a successful immigration lawyer include strong analytical and critical thinking skills, knowledge of immigration law, strong research and writing skills, and the ability to communicate effectively with clients and government officials. They should be able to work independently and be able to work in a team.

The educational path to become an immigration lawyer typically includes a bachelor's degree in any field, followed by a law degree and a license to practice law. Some immigration lawyer positions may also require a master's degree in immigration law or a related field.

The salary for an immigration lawyer can vary depending on factors such as location, employer, and level of experience. According to PayScale, the average salary for an immigration lawyer is around $78,000 per year. However, this can range from around $60,000 to $100,000 per year.

10. Intelligence Analyst

An intelligence analyst is a professional who collects, analyzes, and disseminates information to support decision-making and operations. They may work for a government agency, military organization, or private company. In the context of anti-trafficking, an intelligence analyst would work to gather and analyze information on human trafficking activity and networks. They would also work to identify and assess potential threats and vulnerabilities related to human trafficking, and provide recommendations for action to disrupt and prevent trafficking.

Intelligence analysts play an important role in the fight against human trafficking by gathering and analyzing information on trafficking activity and networks. They help to identify and assess potential threats and vulnerabilities related to human trafficking, and provide recommendations for action to disrupt and prevent trafficking. Through their analysis, intelligence analysts help to provide a more complete understanding of the scope and nature of human trafficking and support efforts to combat it.

The skills required for a successful intelligence analyst include strong analytical and critical thinking skills, knowledge of intelligence analysis techniques, the ability to work with large amounts of data, and the ability to communicate effectively with a variety of stakeholders. They should also have knowledge of human trafficking issues and be able to work independently and as part of a team.

The educational path to become an intelligence analyst typically includes a bachelor's degree in a field such as criminal justice, international relations, or a related field. Some positions may also require a master's degree or specialized training in intelligence analysis.

The salary for an intelligence analyst can vary depending on factors such as location, employer, and level of experience. According to PayScale, the average salary for an intelligence analyst is around $70,000 per year. However, this can range from around $50,000 to $90,000 per year.

11. Law Enforcement Analyst

A law enforcement analyst is a professional who supports law enforcement agencies by providing analysis and research on criminal activity, trends, and patterns. They may work for a government agency, local police department, or private company. In the context of anti-trafficking, a law enforcement analyst would work to provide analysis and research on human trafficking activity, networks, and trends. They would also work to identify and assess potential threats and vulnerabilities related to human trafficking and provide recommendations for action to disrupt and prevent trafficking.

Law enforcement analysts play an important role in the fight against human trafficking by providing analysis and research on trafficking activity, networks, and trends. They help to identify and assess potential threats and vulnerabilities related to human trafficking and provide recommendations for action to disrupt and prevent trafficking. Through their analysis, law enforcement analysts help to provide a more complete understanding of the scope and nature of human trafficking and support efforts to combat it.

The skills required for a successful law enforcement analyst include strong analytical and critical thinking skills, knowledge of criminal activity, trends, and patterns, the ability to work with large amounts of data, and the ability to communicate effectively with law enforcement agencies. They should also have knowledge of human trafficking issues and be able to work independently and as part of a team.

The educational path to become a law enforcement analyst typically includes a bachelor's degree in a field such as criminal justice, criminology, or a related field. Some positions may also require a master's degree or specialized training in law enforcement analysis or a related field.

The salary for a law enforcement analyst can vary depending on factors such as location, employer, and level of experience. According to PayScale, the average salary for a law enforcement analyst is around $57,000 per year. However, this can range from around $45,000 to $70,000 per year. It's important to note that some positions with federal agencies such as the FBI or DEA, may have different requirements and may require more advanced education and experience. Additionally, compensation for these positions may be higher, with salaries ranging from $70,000 to over $100,000 per year.

12. Law Enforcement Officer

A law enforcement officer is a professional who enforces laws and maintains public safety in a community. They may work for a local police department, state police, or federal agency. In the context of anti-trafficking, a law enforcement officer would work to identify, investigate and arrest individuals involved in human trafficking. They would also work to identify and assist victims of trafficking.

Law enforcement officers play a crucial role in the fight against human trafficking by identifying and investigating individuals and organizations involved in human trafficking. They also work to identify and assist victims of trafficking. Through their enforcement efforts, they gather evidence that can be used to prosecute traffickers and disrupt trafficking networks.

The skills required for a successful law enforcement officer include physical fitness, strong communication skills, knowledge of criminal investigation techniques, the ability to work with victims of trauma, and the ability to work with a variety of community members. They should also have knowledge of human trafficking issues and be able to work independently and as part of a team.

The educational path to become a law enforcement officer typically includes a high school diploma or equivalent, and successful completion of a police academy training program. Some agencies may require a college degree in a related field.

The salary for a law enforcement officer can vary depending on factors such as location, employer, and level of experience. According to the Bureau of Labor Statistics, the median annual salary for police and detectives was $65,170 in May 2020. However, this can range from around $40,000 to $100,000 per year.

13. Medical Professional

Medical professionals are healthcare practitioners trained to diagnose, treat, and prevent illnesses and injuries. They may include doctors, nurses, paramedics, and other healthcare professionals. In the context of anti-trafficking, a medical professional would work to provide medical care and support to victims of human trafficking. They would also be responsible for identifying and documenting physical and psychological trauma resulting from trafficking, as well as providing evidence for legal proceedings.

Medical professionals play a critical role in the fight against human trafficking by providing medical care and support to victims. They are also responsible for identifying and documenting physical and psychological trauma resulting from trafficking, as well as providing evidence for legal proceedings. Through their work, medical professionals help to ensure that victims of trafficking receive the care and support they need to begin the process of healing and recovery.

The skills required for a successful medical professional include strong knowledge of human anatomy and physiology, the ability to work with victims of trauma, good communication skills, and the ability to work in a team.

The educational path to become a medical professional varies depending on the specific profession. It typically includes a post-secondary degree in a relevant field and professional training or certification. For example, becoming a doctor requires completing a 4-year undergraduate degree, 4 years of medical school, and 3-7 years of residency and specialty training. While becoming a nurse typically requires a 2-4 year degree and passing the National Council Licensure Examination (NCLEX-RN).

The salary for a medical professional can vary depending on factors such as location, employer, and level of experience. According to the Bureau of Labor Statistics, the median annual salary for physicians and surgeons is $208,000 per year. While the median annual salary for registered nurses is $73,300 per year.

14. Mental Health Counselor

A mental health counselor is a professional who provides therapy and support to individuals experiencing mental health issues. They may work in a private practice, community health center, or hospital. In the context of anti-trafficking, a mental health counselor would work to provide therapy and support to victims of human trafficking. They would also work to identify and address the psychological trauma resulting from trafficking, and help victims to develop coping strategies and resilience.

Mental health counselors play a vital role in the fight against human trafficking by providing therapy and support to victims of trafficking. They help to identify and address the psychological trauma resulting from trafficking and help victims to develop coping strategies and resilience. Through their work, mental health counselors help victims of trafficking to begin the process of healing and recovery.

The skills required for a successful mental health counselor include strong knowledge of mental health disorders, counseling techniques, and intervention strategies, the ability to work with victims of trauma, good communication skills, and the ability to work in a team.

The educational path to become a mental health counselor typically includes a master's degree in counseling or a related field, and licensure or certification as a professional counselor.

The salary for a mental health counselor can vary depending on factors such as location, employer, and level of experience. According to the Bureau of Labor Statistics, the median annual salary for mental health counselors is $48,040 per year. However, this can range from around $35,000 to $70,000 per year.

15.Non-Profit Manager

A non-profit manager is a professional responsible for the overall management and operations of a non-profit organization. They may work in areas such as fundraising, program development, and community outreach. In the context of anti-trafficking, a non-profit manager would work to develop and manage programs aimed at preventing human trafficking and supporting victims of trafficking. They would also be responsible for fundraising and community outreach to raise awareness of human trafficking and support for anti-trafficking efforts.

Non-profit managers play an important role in the fight against human trafficking by developing and managing programs aimed at preventing human trafficking and supporting victims of trafficking. They are also responsible for fundraising and community outreach to raise awareness of human trafficking and support for anti-trafficking efforts. Through their work, non-profit managers help to ensure that resources and support are available to combat trafficking and assist victims.

The skills required for a successful non-profit manager include strong leadership and management skills, the ability to develop and manage programs, knowledge of fundraising and community outreach, and the ability to work with a variety of stakeholders. They should also have knowledge of human trafficking issues and be able to work independently and as part of a team.

The educational path to become a non-profit manager typically includes a bachelor's degree in a related field, such as non-profit management, business administration, or a related field. Some positions may require a master's degree in a related field.

The salary for a non-profit manager can vary depending on factors such as location, employer, and level of experience. According to PayScale, the average salary for a non-profit manager is around $54,000 per year. However, this can range from around $40,000 to $70,000 per year.

16. Public Health Professional

A public health professional is a healthcare practitioner who focuses on the health of communities and populations. They may work in areas such as disease prevention, health promotion, and disaster preparedness. In the context of anti-trafficking, a public health professional would work to identify and address the health needs of victims of human trafficking, and develop and implement programs to prevent trafficking and support victims.

Public health professionals play an important role in the fight against human trafficking by identifying and addressing the health needs of victims of human trafficking, and developing and implementing programs to prevent trafficking and support victims. They work to identify and address the physical and mental health needs of victims, as well as the social determinants of health that may contribute to trafficking. Through their work, public health professionals help to ensure that victims of trafficking receive the care and support they need to begin the process of healing and recovery.

The skills required for a successful public health professional include strong knowledge of public health principles, the ability to work with victims of trauma, good communication skills, and the ability to work in a team. They should also have knowledge of human trafficking issues and be able to work independently and as part of a team.

The educational path to become a public health professional typically includes a master's degree in public health or a related field, such as epidemiology or health promotion.

The salary for a public health professional can vary depending on factors such as location, employer, and level of experience. According to the Bureau of Labor Statistics, the median annual salary for healthcare social workers is $52,810 per year. However, this can range from around $40,000 to $70,000 per year. Salaries can be higher for those with advanced degrees and specialized skills.

17.Public Policy Advocate

A Public Policy Advocate is a professional that works to influence public policy decisions by engaging with government officials, policy makers, and the public. They may work for non-profit organizations, advocacy groups, or government agencies. In the context of anti-trafficking, a Public Policy Advocate would work to raise awareness of human trafficking and advocate for policies and legislation that address the issue. They would also work to mobilize support for anti-trafficking efforts and educate the public about the issue.

Public Policy Advocates play an important role in the fight against human trafficking by raising awareness of human trafficking and advocating for policies and legislation that address the issue. They work to mobilize support for anti-trafficking efforts and educate the public about the issue. Through their work, Public Policy Advocates help to ensure that the issue of human trafficking is addressed in a comprehensive and effective way.

The skills required for a successful Public Policy Advocate include strong knowledge of public policy, the ability to communicate effectively, good research skills, and the ability to work with a variety of stakeholders. They should also have knowledge of human trafficking issues and be able to work independently and as part of a team.

The educational path to become a Public Policy Advocate typically includes a bachelor's degree in a related field, such as political science, sociology, or public administration. Some positions may require a master's degree in a related field.

The salary for a Public Policy Advocate can vary depending on factors such as location, employer, and level of experience. According to Glassdoor, the average salary for a Public Policy Advocate is around $60,000 per year. However, this can range from around $40,000 to $90,000 per year.

18. Program Evaluator

A Program Evaluator is a professional who assesses the effectiveness of programs and initiatives. They may work in a variety of settings, including non-profit organizations, government agencies, and educational institutions. In the context of anti-trafficking, a Program Evaluator would work to assess the effectiveness of anti-trafficking programs and initiatives, and make recommendations for improvement. They would also work to gather data and conduct research to inform the development of new programs and initiatives.

Program Evaluators play an important role in the fight against human trafficking by assessing the effectiveness of anti-trafficking programs and initiatives, and making recommendations for improvement. They gather data and conduct research to inform the development of new programs and initiatives. Through their work, Program Evaluators help to ensure that anti-trafficking efforts are as effective as possible.

The skills required for a successful Program Evaluator include strong research skills, knowledge of program evaluation methods, the ability to analyze data and draw conclusions, and the ability to communicate effectively. They should also have knowledge of human trafficking issues and be able to work independently and as part of a team.

The educational path to become a Program Evaluator typically includes a graduate degree in a related field, such as public administration, sociology, or social work. Some positions may require a PhD.

The salary for a Program Evaluator can vary depending on factors such as location, employer, and level of experience. According to

Glassdoor, the average salary for a Program Evaluator is around $65,000 per year. However, this can range from around $40,000 to $100,000 per year.

19. Researcher

A Researcher is a professional who conducts research in order to gain new knowledge and understanding. They may work in a variety of fields, including academia, government, and industry. In the context of anti-trafficking, a Researcher would work to gather data and conduct research to better understand the issue of human trafficking. They would also work to identify patterns and trends, and make recommendations for interventions and policies to address the issue.

Researchers play an important role in the fight against human trafficking by gathering data and conducting research to better understand the issue. They work to identify patterns and trends, and make recommendations for interventions and policies to address the issue. Through their work, Researchers help to ensure that anti-trafficking efforts are informed by the latest research and understanding of the issue.

The skills required for a successful Researcher include strong research skills, the ability to analyze data, knowledge of research methods, and the ability to communicate effectively. They should also have knowledge of human trafficking issues and be able to work independently and as part of a team.

The educational path to become a Researcher typically includes a graduate degree in a related field, such as sociology, criminology, or public health. Some positions may require a PhD.
The salary for a Researcher can vary depending on factors such as location, employer, and level of experience. According to Glassdoor, the average salary for a Researcher is around $62,000 per year. However, this can range from around $40,000 to $100,000 per year.

20. Social Worker

A Social Worker is a professional who helps individuals, families, and communities to improve their well-being and overall quality of life. They may work in a variety of settings, including schools, hospitals, and government agencies. In the context of anti-trafficking, a Social Worker would work with individuals who have been affected by human trafficking, providing them with support and assistance as they work to rebuild their lives. They would also work to educate the public about human trafficking and advocate for policies and programs to address the issue.

Social Workers play an important role in the fight against human trafficking by providing support and assistance to individuals affected by human trafficking. They work to educate the public about human trafficking and advocate for policies and programs to address the issue. Through their work, Social Workers help to ensure that individuals affected by human trafficking have the support and assistance they need to rebuild their lives.

The skills required for a successful Social Worker include strong communication skills, empathy, problem-solving ability, and the ability to work independently and as part of a team. They should also have knowledge of human trafficking issues and be able to work independently and as part of a team.

The educational path to become a Social Worker typically includes a bachelor's degree in Social Work and also a license to practice as a Social Worker.
The salary for a Social Worker can vary depending on factors such as location, employer, and level of experience. According to Glassdoor, the average salary for a Social Worker is around $50,000 per year. However, this can range from around $40,000 to $70,000 per year.

21.Survivor Advocate

A Survivor Advocate is a professional who works to support individuals who have been affected by human trafficking. They provide a range of services, including emotional support, case management, and assistance in accessing resources such as housing, healthcare, and legal assistance. In addition to working directly with survivors, Survivor Advocates may also work to educate the public about human trafficking, raise awareness about the issue, and advocate for policies and programs to address the issue.

Survivor Advocates play an important role in the fight against human trafficking by providing support and assistance to individuals affected by human trafficking. They work to educate the public about human trafficking and advocate for policies and programs to address the issue. Through their work, Survivor Advocates help to ensure that individuals affected by human trafficking have the support and assistance they need to rebuild their lives.

The skills required for a successful Survivor Advocate include strong communication skills, empathy, problem-solving ability, and the ability to work independently and as part of a team. They should also have knowledge of human trafficking issues and be able to work independently and as part of a team.

The educational path to become a Survivor Advocate can vary, some positions may require a degree in a related field, such as social work or psychology, while others may be open to applicants with a high school diploma or GED. Some organizations may provide on-the-job training for candidates without formal education.

The salary for a Survivor Advocate can vary depending on factors such as location, employer, and level of experience. According to Glassdoor, the average salary for a Survivor Advocate is around $40,000 per year. However, this can range from around $30,000 to $50,000 per year.

22. Trafficking-specific support group facilitator

A Trafficking-specific support group facilitator is a professional who designs, leads, and facilitates support groups for survivors of human trafficking. They are responsible for creating a safe and supportive space for survivors to share their experiences and receive support from their peers. The facilitator may also provide information and resources to help survivors navigate the legal and social service systems, as well as provide support for the unique challenges that trafficking survivors may face.

Trafficking-specific support group facilitators play an important role in the fight against human trafficking by providing critical support and resources to survivors of human trafficking. By creating a safe and supportive space for survivors to share their experiences and receive support from their peers, facilitators can help survivors to cope with the trauma they have experienced and to begin the process of healing and rebuilding their lives.

The skills required for a successful Trafficking-specific support group facilitator include strong communication skills, ability to create a safe and supportive environment, the ability to work with diverse populations, and knowledge of human trafficking issues.

The educational path to become a Trafficking-specific support group facilitator can vary, some positions may require a degree in a related field such as social work, psychology, or counseling, while others may not require a degree but may require certification or training in trauma-informed care and support group facilitation. Salaries for this role can vary depending on the organization and location but typically fall in the range of $30,000 to $50,000 per year.

23. Trainer

A Trainer is a professional who designs and delivers training programs on various topics, including human trafficking. They may provide training to law enforcement, social service providers, and other organizations working to combat human trafficking on topics such as identifying and responding to trafficking victims, understanding the dynamics of trafficking, and implementing effective anti-trafficking policies and procedures.

Trainers play an important role in the fight against human trafficking by educating and building the capacity of organizations and individuals working to combat human trafficking. Through training, they can increase awareness and understanding of human trafficking, improve the ability of organizations to identify and respond to trafficking victims, and promote the implementation of effective anti-trafficking policies and procedures.

The skills required for a successful Trainer include strong communication and presentation skills, the ability to design and deliver effective training programs, and knowledge of human trafficking issues. A background in education or a related field is also beneficial.

The educational path to become a Trainer can vary, some positions may require a degree in a related field such as education or social work, while others may not require a degree but may require certification or training in training and facilitation. Salaries for this role can vary depending on the organization and location but typically fall in the range of $40,000 to $70,000 per year.

24. Victim advocate

A Victim advocate is a professional who provides support and assistance to victims of human trafficking. They may work in a variety of settings, including non-profit organizations, government agencies, and hospitals. Their role involves providing emotional support, connecting victims with resources such as housing, medical care, and legal assistance, and advocating for victims' rights and needs.

Victim advocates play a crucial role in the fight against human trafficking by providing critical support to victims during the recovery process. They help victims to navigate the complex systems and services that are available to them, and work to ensure that victims' rights and needs are respected and met.

The skills required for a successful Victim advocate include strong communication and interpersonal skills, empathy, and the ability to work with individuals from diverse backgrounds. A background in social work, psychology, or a related field is beneficial.

The educational path to become a Victim advocate can vary, some positions may require a degree in a related field such as social work or psychology, while others may not require a degree but may require certification or training in victim advocacy. Salaries for this role can vary depending on the organization and location but typically fall in the range of $30,000 to $60,000 per year.

25. Airline employee

Airline employees, such as flight attendants, gate agents, and pilots, play an important role in the fight against human trafficking. They are often the first line of defense in identifying potential victims of trafficking and alerting the appropriate authorities. They are trained to recognize the signs of trafficking, such as individuals who appear to be under the control of another person, or individuals who seem to be traveling against their will.

Airline employees use their skills to identify and report suspected cases of trafficking to law enforcement and other relevant agencies. They also play a role in providing support and assistance to victims, such as connecting them with resources and providing information about their rights and options.

Skills required for an airline employee include strong communication and interpersonal skills, attention to detail, and the ability to work in a fast-paced and dynamic environment. A background in aviation or transportation may be beneficial.

The educational path to become an airline employee can vary depending on the position, but most positions require a high school diploma or equivalent and on-the-job training. Many airlines also have specific training programs for their employees to recognize and report human trafficking. Salaries for airline employees can vary depending on the position, experience, and location, but flight attendants typically earn around $50,000 to $70,000 per year. Pilots typically earn higher salaries, with a median salary of around $127,000 per year.

26. Business consultant

Business consultants play an important role in the fight against human trafficking by providing expertise and support to businesses to help them identify and address potential trafficking risks in their supply chains. They also advise on best practices to improve transparency and accountability in supply chains and to ensure that products are not made using forced labor or other forms of exploitation.

Business consultants can use their skills in risk assessment, data analysis and research to conduct supply chain audits, assess compliance with legal and ethical standards and identify areas of improvement. They may also work with businesses to develop and implement policies and procedures to combat trafficking, such as training programs for employees and suppliers and protocols for reporting and responding to trafficking concerns.

To be successful as a business consultant, one should have strong analytical and problem-solving skills, knowledge of supply chain management and ethical business practices, and the ability to communicate effectively with clients. A business consultant should also be familiar with laws and regulations related to human trafficking and forced labor.

The educational path to become a business consultant typically includes a bachelor's degree in business, finance, management or a related field. A master's degree in business administration (MBA) or a related field may also be beneficial. Experience in the field of supply chain management or relevant industry is also important. Salaries for business consultants can vary depending on experience and location, with the median salary for management consultants around $85,000 per year. Business consultants may also find themselves working in non-profit organizations, government agencies and international organizations to help combat human trafficking.

27. Business Owner

A business owner is an individual or entity who operates and manages a business. As a business owner, one can play a significant role in combating human trafficking by ensuring that their business does not unknowingly participate in or benefit from trafficking. This can be done by implementing ethical business practices, conducting due diligence on suppliers and vendors, and educating employees on identifying and reporting potential trafficking situations.

To be a successful business owner, one must have strong leadership and management skills, as well as knowledge of the industry in which they operate. There are many paths to becoming a business owner, it can be done through starting a new business, buying an existing business, or becoming a franchisee of an existing business. One can pursue a business degree or take classes on entrepreneurship, but it is not necessary.

The earning potential for a business owner varies greatly depending on the size, industry, and success of the business. According to the Small Business Administration, the average small business owner earns around $75,000 per year. However, it is not uncommon for successful business owners to earn significantly more.

28. Employee Benefits Specialist

An employee benefits specialist is a professional who helps companies design, implement, and administer employee benefits programs such as health insurance, retirement plans, and paid time off. They also educate employees about their benefits, help them enroll in programs, and assist with any questions or issues that may arise.

Employee benefits specialists can play a role in fighting human trafficking by ensuring that companies have policies and procedures in place to prevent trafficking and providing education and resources to employees on how to recognize and report trafficking. They can also use their knowledge of employee benefits to identify potential trafficking victims, such as employees who may not be utilizing their benefits or have unusual requests for time off.

To be an effective employee benefits specialist, one should have strong communication and interpersonal skills, be organized and detail-oriented, and have a good understanding of the laws and regulations related to employee benefits.

To become an employee benefits specialist, a bachelor's degree in a related field such as human resources, business, or finance is often preferred, but it is not always required. Some professionals in this field also hold certifications such as the Certified Employee Benefits Specialist (CEBS) or the Certified Benefits Professional (CBP).

Employee benefits specialists can make a wide range of salary depending on their level of experience and the size and industry of the organization they work for. According to Payscale, the median salary for an employee benefits specialist is $62,000 per year.

29. Entrepreneur

An entrepreneur is someone who starts and runs their own business. They are often the driving force behind new ideas and innovation in the economy. In the fight against human trafficking, entrepreneurs can play a vital role in creating new and innovative solutions to combat the problem.

One way entrepreneurs can be used to fight human trafficking is by creating new technologies or businesses that aim to disrupt and dismantle trafficking networks. For example, an entrepreneur could develop a mobile app that allows people to report suspicious activity or a business that employs survivors of trafficking.

To be successful as an entrepreneur, one must possess a wide range of skills such as creativity, self-motivation, risk management, and business acumen. Additionally, the ability to network and build relationships is crucial for entrepreneurs as they may need to connect with potential investors, customers, and partners.

An entrepreneurial career path can be pursued through a variety of routes, including starting your own business, joining a startup, or working in a corporate entrepreneurship role. While a college degree is not always necessary, many entrepreneurs have a background in business, marketing, or a related field.

The earning potential for entrepreneurs varies greatly, as it is largely dependent on the success of the business. Some entrepreneurs may make very little money, while others may become incredibly successful and wealthy. It is important to note that starting a business is a risky venture and there is a high failure rate, but those who succeed can make a significant income.

30. Financial Analyst

A financial analyst is a professional who conducts research and analysis on financial products and markets to assist in investment decisions. They may work in a variety of settings, such as investment firms, banks, or corporations. In the fight against human trafficking, financial analysts can play a crucial role in identifying and disrupting the financial networks that support trafficking operations.

One way a financial analyst can be used to fight human trafficking is by identifying and tracking suspicious financial transactions. For example, they may analyze bank records or transactions to detect patterns that may indicate trafficking activity. Additionally, they may assist in developing financial sanctions or other measures to disrupt and dismantle trafficking networks.

To be successful as a financial analyst, one must possess strong analytical and critical thinking skills, as well as the ability to interpret and make sense of financial data. Additionally, strong communication skills are important as financial analysts often need to present their findings to others. A knowledge of financial markets and products, as well as accounting principles, is also important.

A career as a financial analyst typically requires at least a bachelor's degree in a field such as finance, economics, or accounting. However, some entry-level positions may be available to those with a degree in a related field such as business or mathematics. Additionally, many employers may require professional certifications such as the Chartered Financial Analyst (CFA) designation.

The earning potential for a financial analyst varies depending on the type of employer, level of experience and geographic location, however, the average salary for a financial analyst is around $80,000

- $110,000. With experience and advancement, financial analysts can earn upwards of $150,000.

31. Fundraiser

A fundraiser is a professional who is responsible for identifying, soliciting and stewarding donations for a non-profit organization, charity or political campaign. They may work in a variety of settings such as non-profit organizations, schools, universities, political campaigns, or charitable foundations. In the fight against human trafficking, fundraisers play an important role in securing the resources needed to support anti-trafficking initiatives and organizations.

One way a fundraiser can be used to fight human trafficking is by identifying and soliciting donations from individuals, foundations and corporations to support anti-trafficking initiatives and organizations. They may also assist in developing grant proposals for government and private foundations to support anti-trafficking projects. Additionally, they may also organize and manage fundraising events such as charity walks, auctions, and galas to raise awareness and funds for anti-trafficking efforts.

To be successful as a fundraiser, one must possess strong communication skills, as well as the ability to build and maintain relationships with donors. They must be able to articulate the mission and goals of an organization and to present compelling cases for support. Additionally, they must have good organizational skills, be able to work independently and be able to work under pressure to meet deadlines and goals.

A career as a fundraiser can be pursued through a variety of routes, including obtaining a degree in nonprofit management, fundraising, marketing, or related field. However, some entry-level positions may be available to those with a degree in a related field such as business, communications, or public relations. Some employers may require professional certifications such as the Certified Fund Raising Executive (CFRE) designation.

The earning potential for a fundraiser varies depending on the type of employer, level of experience and geographic location. However, the average salary for a fundraiser is around $50,000 to $70,000. Some top fundraisers can earn over $100,000 with experience and advancement.

32. Grant Writer

A grant writer is a professional who is responsible for writing and submitting proposals to government agencies, foundations, and other organizations to secure funding for a non-profit organization or project. They may work in a variety of settings such as non-profit organizations, schools, universities, research institutions, or charitable foundations. In the fight against human trafficking, grant writers play an important role in securing the resources needed to support anti-trafficking initiatives and organizations.

One way a grant writer can be used to fight human trafficking is by writing and submitting proposals to government agencies, foundations, and other organizations to secure funding for anti-trafficking initiatives and organizations. They may also assist in developing and maintaining relationships with funders and partners to support anti-trafficking projects. Additionally, they may also research funding opportunities, review and analyze funding guidelines, and develop budgets for proposals.

To be successful as a grant writer, one must have excellent writing skills and the ability to write clear, persuasive and compelling proposals. They must have good research skills, be able to analyze and interpret funding guidelines and be able to work independently and under pressure to meet deadlines. Additionally, they must be able to work effectively with a team and to communicate effectively with funders and partners.

A career as a grant writer can be pursued through a variety of routes, including obtaining a degree in nonprofit management, English, communications, or related field. However, some entry-level positions may be available to those with a degree in a related field such as business, sociology, or public policy. Some employers may require professional certifications such as the Grant Professional Certified (GPC) designation.

The earning potential for a grant writer varies depending on the type of employer, level of experience and geographic location. According to payscale.com, the average salary for a grant writer is around $45,000 to $65,000 per year. With experience and advancement, grant writers can earn upwards of $80,000 per year.

33. Grocery Store Owner

A grocery store owner is an entrepreneur who owns and operates a retail establishment that sells food and household supplies. They may operate a small neighborhood store or a large chain of supermarkets. In the fight against human trafficking, grocery store owners can play an important role in identifying and preventing trafficking within their supply chains and in their communities.

One way grocery store owners can be used to fight human trafficking is by implementing policies and procedures to prevent the use of forced labor in their supply chains. They can also work with local organizations to raise awareness and educate their employees and customers about the issue of human trafficking. Additionally, they can also report suspicious activity to the relevant authorities and participate in anti-trafficking initiatives in the community.

To be successful as a grocery store owner, one must possess strong business acumen and management skills. They should be able to manage the day-to-day operations of the store, including inventory management, financial management, and customer service. Additionally, they must have good communication skills, be able to work independently, and be able to work under pressure to meet deadlines and goals.

An entrepreneurial career path can be pursued through a variety of routes, including starting your own business, joining a startup, or working in a corporate entrepreneurship role. While a college degree is not always necessary, many grocery store owners have a background in business, marketing, or a related field.

The earning potential for a grocery store owner varies greatly, as it is largely dependent on the success of the business. According to IBISWorld, a market research company, the average profit margin for grocery stores is around 2% to 3% of revenue. However, this can vary greatly depending on factors such as location, competition, and scale of the business.

34. Human Resources Professional

A Human Resources (HR) professional is responsible for managing the personnel functions of an organization, including recruiting, hiring, training, and managing employees. They may work in a variety of settings, such as corporations, non-profit organizations, or government agencies. In the fight against human trafficking, HR professionals can play an important role in identifying and preventing trafficking within their organizations and in their communities.

One way an HR professional can be used to fight human trafficking is by implementing policies and procedures to prevent the use of forced labor in their organizations. They can also work with local organizations to raise awareness and educate their employees about the issue of human trafficking. Additionally, they can also report suspicious activity to the relevant authorities and participate in anti-trafficking initiatives in the community.

To be successful as an HR professional, one must possess strong communication and interpersonal skills, as well as the ability to manage and lead teams. They must also have a strong understanding of employment laws and regulations, as well as the ability to analyze and interpret data. Additionally, they must have good organizational skills, be able to work independently, and be able to work under pressure to meet deadlines and goals.

A career in Human Resources can be pursued through a variety of routes, including obtaining a degree in Human Resources, Business Administration, or a related field. However, some entry-level positions may be available to those with a degree in a related field such as psychology, sociology, or communications. Some employers may require professional certifications such as the Senior Professional in Human Resources (SPHR) or the Professional in Human Resources (PHR) designation.

The earning potential for an HR professional varies depending on the type of employer, level of experience and geographic location, however, the average salary for an HR professional is around $60,000 - $100,000. With experience and advancement, some HR professionals can earn upwards of $150,000.

35 Investor

An investor is a person or organization that provides capital to a business or project with the expectation of financial return. They may invest in a variety of assets such as stocks, bonds, real estate, or startups. In the fight against human trafficking, investors can play an important role in identifying and disrupting the financial networks that support trafficking operations and in supporting anti-trafficking initiatives.

One way an investor can be used to fight human trafficking is by investing in companies or projects that aim to combat trafficking. For example, an investor could fund a technology startup that develops a platform to track and report suspicious activity or invest in a business that employs survivors of trafficking. Additionally, they can also use their influence to encourage companies in which they are invested to adopt policies and practices that prevent trafficking in their supply chains.

To be successful as an investor, one must possess strong analytical and critical thinking skills, as well as the ability to interpret and make sense of financial data. Additionally, strong communication and negotiation skills are important as investors often need to present their investment thesis to others and negotiate investment terms. A good understanding of financial markets and products is also important.

An investment career can be pursued through a variety of routes, including working for an investment bank, hedge fund, private equity firm, or as an independent investor. A college degree is not always necessary, but many investors have a background in finance, economics, or a related field. Additionally, many employers may require professional certifications such as the Chartered Financial Analyst (CFA) designation.

The earning potential for an investor varies greatly, as it is largely dependent on the success of the investments. Some investors may make very little money, while others may become incredibly successful and wealthy. However, according to payscale.com, the average salary for an investor is around $80,000 to $150,000 per year. With experience and advancement, investors can earn over $500,000 per year.

36. Philanthropist

A philanthropist is a person who actively engages in philanthropy, which is the act of giving money, time, or resources to support a cause or organization. Philanthropists may give to a wide range of causes, including education, health care, poverty, and human rights. In the fight against human trafficking, philanthropists can play an important role in providing resources and support to organizations and initiatives that work to combat trafficking.

One way a philanthropist can be used to fight human trafficking is by providing financial support to organizations and initiatives that work to combat trafficking, such as NGOs, shelters, and hotlines. They can also use their influence and connections to raise awareness and advocate for anti-trafficking policies and practices. Additionally, they can also use their resources to establish and support programs that provide services and support to survivors of trafficking.

To be successful as a philanthropist, one must possess a strong passion and commitment to a cause, as well as the ability to identify and evaluate organizations and initiatives that align with their values and goals. Additionally, strong communication and networking skills are important as philanthropists often need to connect with organizations and other individuals to build partnerships and support for their causes.

A career as a philanthropist does not require a specific educational path, as many philanthropists come from a variety of backgrounds and careers. However, some philanthropists may have a background in business, law, or a related field. Additionally, some philanthropists may choose to pursue formal education in fields such as nonprofit management or philanthropy.

The earning potential for a philanthropist varies greatly, as it is largely dependent on their personal wealth and resources. Philanthropists can make a significant impact through their giving, regardless of their income level. However, some of the wealthiest philanthropists in the world have donated millions or even billions of dollars to charitable causes.

37. Port Worker

A port worker is a person who works in a port, which is an area of water where ships can load and unload cargo. Port workers can have a variety of roles, such as dockworkers, crane operators, or freight handlers. In the fight against human trafficking, port workers can play an important role in identifying and preventing trafficking in the shipping industry.

One way a port worker can be used to fight human trafficking is by being aware of the signs of trafficking and reporting suspicious activity to the relevant authorities. They can also work with organizations and agencies to raise awareness and educate their colleagues about the issue of human trafficking. Additionally, they can also support anti-trafficking initiatives and policies implemented by the port or shipping company they work for.

To be successful as a port worker, one must be physically fit and able to lift heavy cargo, have good hand-eye coordination and be able to work in a fast-paced environment. Additionally, they must have good communication skills and be able to work as part of a team. Knowledge of shipping procedures and regulations is also important.

A career as a port worker does not require a specific educational path, as many port workers have a high school diploma or equivalent. However, some employers may require a commercial driver's license or specialized training for certain roles. Additionally, some employers may provide on-the-job training for entry-level positions.

The earning potential for a port worker varies depending on the type of employer, level of experience and geographic location. According to payscale.com, the average salary for a port worker is around $35,000 to $50,000 per year. However, it can be higher for those with specialized roles or who work in larger ports.

38. Recruiter

A Recruiter is a professional responsible for identifying, recruiting, and hiring candidates for an organization. They may work in a variety of settings such as corporations, staffing agencies, or non-profit organizations. In the fight against human trafficking, recruiters can play an important role in identifying and preventing trafficking within the recruitment process and in the workplace.

One way a Recruiter can be used to fight human trafficking is by implementing policies and procedures to prevent the use of forced labor in the recruitment process. They can also work with local organizations to raise awareness and educate their colleagues and candidates about the issue of human trafficking. Additionally, they can also report suspicious activity to the relevant authorities and participate in anti-trafficking initiatives in the community.

To be successful as a Recruiter, one must possess strong communication and interpersonal skills, as well as the ability to manage and lead teams. They must also have a strong understanding of employment laws and regulations, as well as the ability to analyze and interpret data. Additionally, they must have good organizational skills, be able to work independently, and be able to work under pressure to meet deadlines and goals.

A career as a Recruiter can be pursued through a variety of routes, including obtaining a degree in Human Resources, Business Administration, or a related field. However, some entry-level positions may be available to those with a degree in a related field such as psychology, sociology, or communications. Some employers may require professional certifications such as the National Recruiter Certification (NRC) or the Certified Recruiting Professional (CRP) designation.

The earning potential for a Recruiter varies depending on the type of employer, level of experience and geographic location. According to payscale.com, the average salary for a Recruiter is around $45,000 to $65,000 per year. With experience and advancement, recruiters can earn upwards of $80,000 to $100,000 per year. Additionally, recruiters who work on a commission-based structure can earn even more, depending on the number and success of their placements.

39. Specialty Food Store Owner

A Specialty Food Store Owner is an entrepreneur who owns and operates a retail establishment that sells specialty foods such as gourmet, organic, and local foods. They may operate a small neighborhood store or a chain of specialty food stores. In the fight against human trafficking, Specialty Food Store Owners can play an important role in identifying and preventing trafficking within their supply chains and in their communities.

One way a Specialty Food Store Owner can be used to fight human trafficking is by implementing policies and procedures to prevent the use of forced labor in their supply chains. They can also work with local organizations to raise awareness and educate their employees and customers about the issue of human trafficking. Additionally, they can also report suspicious activity to the relevant authorities and participate in anti-trafficking initiatives in the community.

To be successful as a Specialty Food Store Owner, one must possess strong business acumen and management skills. They should be able to manage the day-to-day operations of the store, including inventory management, financial management, and customer service. Additionally, they must have good communication skills, be able to work independently, and be able to work under pressure to meet deadlines and goals. A passion for food and knowledge of specialty food products is also important.

An entrepreneurial career path can be pursued through a variety of routes, including starting your own business, joining a startup, or working in a corporate entrepreneurship role. While a college degree is not always necessary, many Specialty Food Store Owners have a background in business, marketing, or a related field. Additionally, some may have a background in culinary arts or food industry.

The earning potential for a Specialty Food Store Owner varies greatly, as it is largely dependent on the success of the business. However, according to IBISWorld, a market research company, the average profit margin for specialty food stores is around 4% to 5% of revenue. However, this can vary greatly depending on factors such as location, competition, and scale of the business.

40. Supply Chain Professional

A Supply Chain Professional is a person who works in the logistics and coordination of the movement of goods from the manufacturer to the consumer. They may work in a variety of settings such as manufacturing, retail, or logistics companies. In the fight against human trafficking, Supply Chain Professionals can play an important role in identifying and preventing trafficking within the supply chains of their organizations and in their communities.

One way a Supply Chain Professional can be used to fight human trafficking is by implementing policies and procedures to prevent the use of forced labor in their supply chains. They can also work with local organizations to raise awareness and educate their colleagues about the issue of human trafficking. Additionally, they can also report suspicious activity to the relevant authorities and participate in anti-trafficking initiatives in the community.

To be successful as a Supply Chain Professional, one must possess strong analytical and critical thinking skills, as well as the ability to interpret and make sense of logistics data. Additionally, strong communication and negotiation skills are important as supply chain professionals often need to present their supply chain plans to others and negotiate logistics terms. A good understanding of supply chain management and logistics is also important.

A career in Supply Chain Management can be pursued through a variety of routes, including obtaining a degree in Supply Chain Management, Business Administration, or a related field. However, some entry-level positions may be available to those with a degree in a related field such as engineering, mathematics, or computer science. Some employers may require professional certifications such as the Certified Supply Chain Professional (CSCP) or the Certified in Logistics, Transportation, and Distribution (CLTD) designation.

The earning potential for a Supply Chain Professional varies depending on the type of employer, level of experience, and geographic location. According to payscale.com, the average salary for a Supply Chain Professional is around $60,000 to $90,000 per year. With experience and advancement, supply chain professionals can earn upwards of $100,000 to $150,000 per year.

41. Talent Acquisition Specialist

A Talent Acquisition Specialist is a professional who specializes in identifying, recruiting, and hiring top talent for an organization. They may work in a variety of settings such as corporations, staffing agencies, or non-profit organizations. In the fight against human trafficking, Talent Acquisition Specialists can play an important role in identifying and preventing trafficking within the recruitment process and in the workplace.

One way a Talent Acquisition Specialist can be used to fight human trafficking is by implementing policies and procedures to prevent the use of forced labor in the recruitment process. They can also work with local organizations to raise awareness and educate their colleagues and candidates about the issue of human trafficking. Additionally, they can also report suspicious activity to the relevant authorities and participate in anti-trafficking initiatives in the community.

To be successful as a Talent Acquisition Specialist, one must possess strong communication and interpersonal skills, as well as the ability to manage and lead teams. They must also have a strong understanding of employment laws and regulations, as well as the ability to analyze and interpret data. Additionally, they must have good organizational skills, be able to work independently, and be able to work under pressure to meet deadlines and goals.

A career as a Talent Acquisition Specialist can be pursued through a variety of routes, including obtaining a degree in Human Resources, Business Administration, or a related field. However, some entry-level positions may be available to those with a degree in a related field such as psychology, sociology, or communications. Some employers may require professional certifications such as the National Recruiter Certification (NRC) or the Certified Recruiting Professional (CRP) designation.

The earning potential for a Talent Acquisition Specialist varies depending on the type of employer, level of experience, and geographic location. According to payscale.com, the average salary for a Talent Acquisition Specialist is around $50,000 to $70,000 per year. With experience and advancement, Talent Acquisition Specialists can earn upwards of $80,000 to $100,000 per year. Additionally, Talent Acquisition Specialists who work on a commission-based structure can earn even more, depending on the number and success of their placements.

42. Activist

An activist is a person who actively campaigns for a social or political cause. They work to raise awareness about issues and to bring about change through protests, demonstrations, and other forms of direct action. Activists can be involved in a wide range of causes, including anti-trafficking efforts.

Activists can play an important role in the fight against human trafficking by raising awareness about the issue, lobbying for policy changes, and supporting survivors. They can organize protests, write letters to government officials, and work with other organizations to bring attention to the problem of human trafficking. Activists can also work to change laws and policies that make it easier for traffickers to operate, and they can support survivors by providing them with resources and helping them to access services.

To be an effective activist, it is important to have strong communication skills, both written and verbal. Activists should also be well-informed about the issue they are campaigning for, and be able to persuasively communicate their message to others. Strong leadership and organizational skills are also important for activists, as they often need to coordinate and mobilize groups of people to achieve their goals.

A formal education is not required to become an activist, but many people who are active in social and political causes have at least a bachelor's degree. Some activists may have degrees in fields like political science, sociology, or law, but others may have degrees in unrelated fields.

The salary of an activist varies widely depending on the type of organization they work for and their level of experience. Some activists may be paid a salary by a non-profit organization, while others may volunteer their time. Activists who are self-employed or working for a small organization may earn less than those working for a larger organization with more funding. Some activists may also receive stipends or travel reimbursements for their work.

43. Community leader

A community leader is a person who is respected and influential within a particular community. They may hold formal positions of leadership, such as serving on a community board or council, or they may be informal leaders who are recognized for their knowledge, skills, and dedication to the community. Community leaders can play an important role in the fight against human trafficking by raising awareness about the issue and supporting survivors.

Community leaders can be involved in anti-trafficking efforts by educating their community about the signs of trafficking, such as a lack of identification or control over their own movement. They can also advocate for policies and services that support survivors of trafficking, such as providing them with housing, healthcare, and job training. Community leaders can also work with local law enforcement and other organizations to establish a response plan for identifying and assisting survivors.

To be an effective community leader, it is important to have strong communication skills, be able to work well with others, and have a deep understanding of the community you serve. They should also be knowledgeable about the issue of human trafficking, and be able to persuasively communicate the importance of addressing it. Leadership and organizational skills are also important for community leaders, as they often need to coordinate and mobilize groups of people to achieve their goals.

A formal education is not required to become a community leader, but many people who are active in their community have at least a high school diploma. Some community leaders may have degrees in fields like social work, public health, or public policy, but others may have degrees in unrelated fields.

The salary of a community leader varies widely depending on the type of organization they work for and their level of experience. Some community leaders may be paid a salary by a non-profit organization, while others may volunteer their time. Community leaders who are self-employed or working for a small organization may earn less than those working for a larger organization with more funding. Some community leaders may also receive stipends or travel reimbursements for their work.

44. Event Planner

An event planner is a professional who is responsible for organizing and coordinating events such as conferences, conventions, and fundraisers. They handle all aspects of event planning, from researching and selecting venues, to coordinating speakers, vendors, and attendees. Event planners can play an important role in the fight against human trafficking by organizing events that raise awareness about the issue and raise funds for anti-trafficking organizations.

Event planners can support anti-trafficking efforts by organizing events such as fundraisers, conferences, and awareness-raising campaigns. They can also collaborate with other organizations, such as non-profits, to plan and execute events that will help to educate the public about human trafficking and raise funds to support survivors. They can also work with law enforcement and other professionals to develop strategies for identifying and responding to trafficking victims.

To be an effective event planner, it is important to have strong organizational and project management skills. They should also have good communication skills and the ability to work well with a wide range of people, including vendors, sponsors, and attendees. Strong attention to detail and the ability to work well under pressure is also essential.

A formal education is not required to become an event planner, but many event planners have at least an associate's degree in event planning, hospitality management, or a related field. Some also have a degree in marketing, business, or communications. On the job training and experience are also important for an event planner.

The salary of an event planner varies widely depending on their level of experience, the size of the company they work for, and the type of events they plan. Entry-level event planners can earn around $30,000 to $40,000 per year, while more experienced planners can earn upwards of $70,000. Self-employed event planners can charge a fee for their services, which can vary depending on the event and the client.

45.Filmmaker

A filmmaker is a person who creates films, whether for commercial, artistic or educational purposes. They are responsible for the visual and audio elements of a film, including writing, directing, and producing. Filmmakers can play an important role in the fight against human trafficking by creating films that raise awareness about the issue and educate the public about the realities of trafficking.

Filmmakers can support anti-trafficking efforts by creating films that explore the issue of human trafficking from a variety of perspectives.

They can create documentaries, feature films, and short films that reveal the complexities of trafficking, and expose the injustices suffered by victims. They can also create public service announcements and educational videos that inform the public about the signs of trafficking and how to report it.

To be an effective filmmaker, one should have strong storytelling and visual storytelling skills, be able to collaborate with different people, have knowledge of film production techniques and equipment, and have good communication skills. They should also have a deep understanding of the issue of human trafficking and be able to communicate it effectively.

A formal education is not required to become a filmmaker, but many successful filmmakers have a degree in film or a related field such as film production, film studies, or television production. However, on the job training and experience is also important for a filmmaker.

The salary of a filmmaker can vary widely depending on the type of films they create, their level of experience, and the size of the company they work for. Independent filmmakers may earn less than those working for a large studio, but can also have more creative control over their work. Many filmmakers are freelance, and their income will depend on the number and size of the projects they take on. However, the median salary for a filmmaker is around $62,000 per year.

46. Fundraiser

A fundraiser is a professional who is responsible for generating financial support for organizations and causes. They may work for non-profit organizations, political campaigns, or charitable causes. Fundraisers can play an important role in the fight against human trafficking by raising money for organizations that provide services and support for survivors.

Fundraisers can support anti-trafficking efforts by organizing events and campaigns that raise money for organizations that provide services and support for survivors. They can also work with donors, foundations, and corporations to secure funding for these organizations. Additionally, they may work with other organizations to create and implement fundraising strategies that align with the mission of the organization and help to achieve the goal of fighting human trafficking.

To be an effective fundraiser, it is important to have strong communication skills and be able to work well with a wide range of people, including donors, volunteers, and staff. They should also have a good understanding of the issue of human trafficking and be able to effectively communicate the importance of supporting organizations that provide services and support for survivors. Strong organizational and project management skills, as well as creativity and the ability to think outside the box are also important for a fundraiser.

A formal education is not required to become a fundraiser, but many successful fundraisers have a degree in a related field such as non-profit management, marketing, communications or business. However, on the job training and experience is also important for a fundraiser.

The salary of a fundraiser can vary widely depending on the type of organization they work for, their level of experience, and the size of the organization. According to the Bureau of Labor Statistics, the median annual salary for fundraisers is $56,790, with the top 10% earning more than $94,860. However, it's worth noting that some fundraisers may work on a commission basis, and their income will depend on the amount of funds they are able to raise for the organization.

47.Graphic Designer

A graphic designer is a professional who creates visual concepts, using computer software or by hand, to communicate ideas that inspire, inform, or captivate consumers. They work on a variety of projects such as websites, brochures, posters, and packaging. Graphic designers can play an important role in the fight against human trafficking by creating visual materials that raise awareness about the issue and educate the public about the realities of trafficking.

Graphic designers can support anti-trafficking efforts by creating visual materials such as posters, brochures, and infographics that inform the public about the signs of trafficking and how to report it. They can also work with other organizations to create materials that raise awareness about the issue and educate the public about the realities of trafficking. They can also work with law enforcement and other professionals to develop strategies for identifying and responding to trafficking victims.

To be an effective graphic designer, it is important to have strong design skills, be able to work well with a wide range of people, have knowledge of graphic design software and techniques, and have a good understanding of the issue of human trafficking. They should also be able to effectively communicate the importance of addressing it through visual means.

A formal education is not required to become a graphic designer, but many successful graphic designers have a degree in graphic design or a related field. However, on the job training and experience is also important for a graphic designer.

The salary of a graphic designer can vary widely depending on their level of experience, the size of the company they work for, and the type of projects they work on. According to the Bureau of Labor Statistics, the median annual salary for graphic designers is $52,110, with the top 10% earning more than $86,500. However, it's worth noting that some graphic designers may work on a freelance or contract basis, and their income will depend on the number and size of the projects they take on.

48. Journalist

A journalist is a professional who gathers, writes, and reports on news and current events for various mediums such as newspapers, magazines, television, and online publications. They may specialize in specific types of journalism such as investigative, political or feature journalism. Journalists can play an important role in the fight against human trafficking by raising awareness about the issue and educating the public about the realities of trafficking.

Journalists can support anti-trafficking efforts by investigating and reporting on the issue of human trafficking. They can write articles, create documentaries, and produce segments for television and radio that inform the public about the signs of trafficking, the impact on survivors, and the efforts being made to combat it. They can also work with other organizations to create materials that raise awareness about the issue and educate the public about the realities of trafficking.

To be an effective journalist, it is important to have strong research and writing skills, be able to work well under pressure and with tight deadlines, have knowledge of the issue of human trafficking, be able to effectively communicate the importance of addressing it, and be able to work well with a wide range of people.

A formal education is not required to become a journalist, but many successful journalists have a degree in journalism or a related field such as English, Communications, or Media Studies. However, on the job training and experience is also important for a journalist.

The salary of a journalist can vary widely depending on the type of organization they work for, their level of experience, and the size of the organization. According to the Bureau of Labor Statistics, the median annual salary for journalists is $46,270, with the top 10% earning more than $89,780. However, it's worth noting that the salary can vary greatly based on the type of journalism they specialize in, and whether they work for a newspaper, magazine, television station, or online publication. Additionally, the salary can also vary based on the location and size of the market they work in. Some journalists may also work on a freelance or contract basis, and their income will depend on the number and size of the projects they take on.

49. Lobbyist

A lobbyist is a professional who works to influence legislation and public policy on behalf of a specific interest group, such as a corporation, trade association, or non-profit organization. They may work in a variety of settings, such as government, private business, or non-profit organizations. Lobbyists can play an important role in the fight against human trafficking by advocating for laws and policies that support survivors and help to combat trafficking.

Lobbyists can support anti-trafficking efforts by advocating for laws and policies that support survivors and help to combat trafficking. They may work with legislators and government officials to draft and pass laws and policies that address trafficking, such as laws that increase penalties for traffickers and provide services and support for survivors. They may also work with other organizations to create and implement advocacy strategies that align with the mission of the organization and the goal of fighting human trafficking.

To be an effective lobbyist, it is important to have strong communication and interpersonal skills, be able to work well with a wide range of people, have knowledge of the issue of human trafficking, and be able to effectively communicate the importance of addressing it through laws and policies. Strong research, analytical and strategic thinking skills are also important for a lobbyist.

A formal education is not required to become a lobbyist, but many successful lobbyists have a degree in a related field such as political science, law, or public policy. However, on the job training and experience is also important for a lobbyist.

The salary of a lobbyist can vary widely depending on the type of organization they work for, their level of experience, and the size of the organization. According to the Bureau of Labor Statistics, the median annual salary for lobbyists is $68,810, with the top 10% earning more than $187,199. However, it's worth noting that the salary can vary greatly based on the type of lobbying they specialize in, and whether they work for a government agency, private business, or non-profit organization. Additionally, the salary can also vary based on the location and size of the market they work in. Some lobbyists may also work on a freelance or contract basis, and their income will depend on the number and size of the projects they take on.

50. Media Specialist

A media specialist is a professional who is responsible for managing the communication and media strategies of an organization. They may work for a variety of organizations such as non-profits, corporations, government agencies, and political campaigns. Media specialists can play an important role in the fight against human trafficking by creating and implementing communication strategies that raise awareness about the issue and educate the public about the realities of trafficking.

Media specialists can support anti-trafficking efforts by creating and implementing communication strategies that raise awareness about the issue of human trafficking and educate the public about the signs of trafficking and how to report it. They can work with other organizations to create and distribute materials such as press releases, videos, and social media posts that inform the public about the issue and the efforts being made to combat it. They may also work with law enforcement and other professionals to develop strategies for identifying and responding to trafficking victims.

To be an effective media specialist, it is important to have strong communication skills, be able to work well with a wide range of people, have knowledge of the issue of human trafficking, be able to effectively communicate the importance of addressing it, and have knowledge of various forms of media and how to use them. Strong organizational and project management skills are also important for a media specialist.

A formal education is not required to become a media specialist, but many successful media specialists have a degree in a related field such as Communications, Public Relations, or Marketing. However, on the job training and experience is also important for a media specialist.

The salary of a media specialist can vary widely depending on the type of organization they work for, their level of experience, and the size of the organization. According to the Bureau of Labor Statistics, the median annual salary for media specialists is $58,850, with the top 10% earning more than $119,610. However, it's worth noting that the salary can vary greatly based on the type of media they specialize in and the location and size of the market they work in.

51. Philanthropy Professional

A philanthropy professional is a professional who is responsible for managing the philanthropic efforts of an organization or individual. They may work for a variety of organizations such as non-profits, foundations, or corporations. Philanthropy professionals can play an important role in the fight against human trafficking by identifying and securing funding for organizations that provide services and support for survivors.

Philanthropy professionals can support anti-trafficking efforts by identifying funding sources and working with donors, foundations, and corporations to secure funding for organizations that provide services and support for survivors. They may also work with other organizations to create and implement philanthropic strategies that align with the mission of the organization and the goal of fighting human trafficking.

To be an effective philanthropy professional, it is important to have strong communication and interpersonal skills, be able to work well with a wide range of people, have knowledge of the issue of human trafficking, be able to effectively communicate the importance of addressing it, and have knowledge of philanthropic trends and funding sources. Strong research, analytical and strategic thinking skills are also important for a philanthropy professional.

A formal education is not required to become a philanthropy professional, but many successful philanthropy professionals have a degree in a related field such as non-profit management, business, or public administration. However, on the job training and experience is also important for a philanthropy professional.

The salary of a philanthropy professional can vary widely depending on the type of organization they work for, their level of experience, and the size of the organization. According to the Bureau of Labor Statistics, the median annual salary for fundraisers is $56,790, with the top 10% earning more than $94,860. However, it's worth noting that the salary can vary greatly based on the type of organization they work for, their level of experience and the location and size of the market they work in.

52. Photographer

A photographer is a professional who captures still images using a camera and various techniques to create visually pleasing and meaningful photographs. They may specialize in various fields such as portrait, commercial, or journalistic photography. Photographers can play an important role in the fight against human trafficking by creating visual materials that raise awareness about the issue and educate the public about the realities of trafficking.

Photographers can support anti-trafficking efforts by capturing images that inform the public about the issue of human trafficking and the impact it has on survivors. They may take photographs of survivors, advocates, and organizations that provide services and support for survivors. They can also work with other organizations to create visual materials such as posters, brochures, and infographics that inform the public about the signs of trafficking and how to report it. They can also work with law enforcement and other professionals to develop strategies for identifying and responding to trafficking victims.

To be an effective photographer, it is important to have strong technical skills in photography, be able to work well with a wide range of people, have knowledge of the issue of human trafficking, be able to effectively communicate the importance of addressing it, and be able to work well under pressure and with tight deadlines.

A formal education is not required to become a photographer, but many successful photographers have a degree in photography or a related field such as fine arts or visual communications. However, on the job training and experience is also important for a photographer.

The salary of a photographer can vary widely depending on the type of photography they specialize in, their level of experience, and the size of the organization. According to the Bureau of Labor Statistics, the median annual salary for photographers is $34,000. However, it's worth noting that the salary can vary greatly based on the type of photography they specialize in, and whether they work for a studio, newspaper, magazine, television station, or work as a freelance photographer. Additionally, the salary can also vary based on the location and size of the market they work in. Some photographers may also work on a freelance or contract basis, and their income will depend on the number and size of the projects they take on.

53. Pollster

A pollster is a professional who designs and conducts surveys to gather public opinion on various topics. They may work for a variety of organizations such as government agencies, political campaigns, market research firms or consulting companies. Pollsters can play an important role in the fight against human trafficking by gathering data and insights that inform policies and programs to combat trafficking.

Pollsters can support anti-trafficking efforts by conducting surveys and research to gather data on the prevalence of human trafficking in a particular area and the attitudes of the general public towards the issue. They can also work with organizations to gather data on the effectiveness of anti-trafficking policies and programs, and use this data to inform the development of new policies and programs. They can also conduct surveys on the awareness and perception of human trafficking among the general public, which can be used to develop more effective public awareness and education campaigns.

To be an effective pollster, it is important to have strong analytical and research skills, be able to work well with a wide range of people, have knowledge of the issue of human trafficking, be able to effectively communicate the importance of addressing it, and have knowledge of survey design and data analysis methods. Strong communication and presentation skills are also important for a pollster.

A formal education is not required to become a pollster, but many successful pollsters have a degree in a related field such as statistics, sociology, psychology or political science. However, on the job training and experience is also important for a pollster.

The salary of a pollster can vary widely depending on the type of organization they work for, their level of experience, and the size of the organization. According to the Bureau of Labor Statistics, the median annual salary for survey researchers is $57,700, with the top 10% earning more than $115,320. However, it's worth noting that the salary can vary greatly based on the type of research they specialize in and the location and size of the market they work in.

54. Political Campaign Worker

A political campaign worker is a professional who works on a political campaign to support a candidate or party in an election. They may work on various aspects of a campaign such as fundraising, voter outreach, and campaign strategy. Political campaign workers can play an important role in the fight against human trafficking by advocating for candidates and policies that support survivors and help to combat trafficking.

Political campaign workers can support anti-trafficking efforts by working on campaigns that advocate for candidates and policies that support survivors and help to combat trafficking. They may work with legislators and government officials to draft and pass laws and policies that address trafficking, such as laws that increase penalties for traffickers and provide services and support for survivors. They may also work with other organizations to create and implement advocacy strategies that align with the mission of the organization and the goal of fighting human trafficking.

To be an effective political campaign worker, it is important to have strong communication and interpersonal skills, be able to work well with a wide range of people, have knowledge of the issue of human trafficking, be able to effectively communicate the importance of addressing it, and have knowledge of the political process and campaign strategy. Strong organizational and project management skills are also important for a political campaign worker.

A formal education is not required to become a political campaign worker, but many successful political campaign workers have a degree in a related field such as political science, law, or public policy. However, on the job training and experience is also important for a political campaign worker.

The salary of a political campaign worker can vary widely depending on the type of campaign they work for, their level of experience, and the size of the organization. According to the Bureau of Labor Statistics, the median annual salary for political campaign workers is not available. However, it's worth noting that the salary can vary greatly based on the type of campaign they work for, their level of experience, and the location and size of the market they work in. Many political campaign workers are volunteers and do not get paid, but some may get a stipend or salary from the campaign or organization they are working for.

55.Public Official

A public official is an elected or appointed official who holds a position within a government agency or department. They may hold positions such as mayor, governor, congressperson, or judge. Public officials can play an important role in the fight against human trafficking by creating and implementing policies and programs that address trafficking and support survivors.

Public officials can support anti-trafficking efforts by creating and implementing policies and programs that address trafficking and support survivors. They may work with other organizations to draft and pass laws that increase penalties for traffickers and provide services and support for survivors. They may also work with law enforcement and other professionals to develop strategies for identifying and responding to trafficking victims. They may also be involved in budget allocation and management for anti-trafficking programs and services.

To be an effective public official, it is important to have strong communication and interpersonal skills, be able to work well with a wide range of people, have knowledge of the issue of human trafficking, be able to effectively communicate the importance of addressing it, and have knowledge of the political process and government policies. Strong analytical and strategic thinking skills are also important for a public official.

Becoming a public official typically requires a college degree, although the specific field of study is not always relevant. They are often elected by the public or appointed by the governor or other high-ranking officials. They may also need to meet certain qualifications such as being a resident of the state or district they wish to represent, being a certain age, and being a registered voter of the political party they are running for. Additionally, it is often helpful for public officials to have prior experience working in government or politics, such as working on a campaign, working as a legislative aide, or working in a government agency.

The salary of a public official can vary widely depending on the level of government and the specific position they hold. According to the Bureau of Labor Statistics, the median annual salary for legislators is $49,630, with the top 10% earning more than $90,930. However, it's worth noting that the salary can vary greatly based on the level of government they work for and the location and size of the market they work in. Additionally, some public officials, particularly those at the state and local level, may receive a smaller salary and may have other sources of income.

56. Public Opinion Researcher

A public opinion researcher is a professional who designs, conducts and analyzes surveys and research to understand public opinion on various topics. They may work for a variety of organizations such as government agencies, political campaigns, market research firms or consulting companies. Public opinion researchers can play an important role in the fight against human trafficking by gathering data and insights that inform policies and programs to combat trafficking.

Public opinion researchers can support anti-trafficking efforts by conducting surveys and research to gather data on the public's perception and awareness of human trafficking. They can also work with organizations to gather data on the effectiveness of anti-trafficking policies and programs, and use this data to inform the development of new policies and programs. They can also conduct surveys on the public's attitudes towards victims of human trafficking and their willingness to support anti-trafficking efforts. They can also conduct focus groups and in-depth interviews to gain a deeper understanding of the public's perceptions of human trafficking.

To be an effective public opinion researcher, it is important to have strong analytical and research skills, be able to work well with a wide range of people, have knowledge of the issue of human trafficking, be able to effectively communicate the importance of addressing it, and have knowledge of survey design and data analysis methods. Strong communication and presentation skills are also important for a public opinion researcher.

A formal education is often required to become a public opinion researcher, many successful public opinion researchers have a degree in a related field such as statistics, sociology, psychology or political science. However, on the job training and experience is also important for a public opinion researcher.

The salary of a public opinion researcher can vary widely depending on the type of organization they work for, their level of experience, and the size of the organization. According to the Bureau of Labor Statistics, the median annual salary for survey researchers is $57,700, with the top 10% earning more than $115,320. However, it's worth noting that the salary can vary greatly based on the type of research they specialize in and the location and size of the market they work in.

57. Public Speaker

A public speaker is an individual who delivers speeches, presentations or talks to an audience on various topics. They may work for a variety of organizations such as non-profits, government agencies, corporations, or as independent speakers. Public speakers can play an important role in the fight against human trafficking by raising awareness and educating the public about the issue.

Public speakers can support anti-trafficking efforts by speaking to various groups and organizations about the issue of human trafficking. They can educate the public about the signs of trafficking, the impact it has on victims and society, and the steps that can be taken to combat it. They can also raise awareness about the issue by speaking at conferences, events, and rallies. They can also speak to government officials, law enforcement agencies and other organizations about the importance of addressing human trafficking.

To be an effective public speaker, it is important to have strong communication and interpersonal skills, be able to work well with a wide range of people, have knowledge of the issue of human trafficking, be able to effectively communicate the importance of addressing it, and have the ability to engage and inspire the audience. Strong research and analytical skills are also important for a public speaker to effectively build the content of their speeches.

A formal education is not always required to become a public speaker, but many successful public speakers have a degree in a related field such as communication, public relations, or political science. However, on the job training and experience is also important for a public speaker.

The salary of a public speaker can vary widely depending on their level of experience, reputation and the type of events and organizations they speak to. According to the Bureau of Labor Statistics, the median annual salary for self-employed speakers is $62,500, with the top 10% earning more than $121,000. However, it's worth noting that the salary can vary greatly based on the type of speaking engagements they specialize in and the location and size of the market they work in. Many public speakers also receive income from other sources such as book sales,

58. Religious Leader

A religious leader is an individual who is responsible for leading religious ceremonies and providing spiritual guidance to their followers. They may hold positions such as a minister, priest, imam, or rabbi. Religious leaders can play an important role in the fight against human trafficking by raising awareness and educating their congregations about the issue.

Religious leaders can support anti-trafficking efforts by educating their congregations about the issue of human trafficking, the signs of trafficking and the impact it has on victims and society. They can also provide spiritual guidance and support to survivors of trafficking. They can also work with other organizations to provide safe spaces and resources for victims and survivors.

They can also raise awareness about the issue by speaking at conferences, events, and rallies.

To be an effective religious leader, it is important to have strong communication and interpersonal skills, be able to work well with a wide range of people, have knowledge of the issue of human trafficking, be able to effectively communicate the importance of addressing it, and have deep understanding of their religion and the principles that guide it. Strong leadership skills are also important for a religious leader to effectively guide and support their congregations.

Becoming a religious leader typically requires a college degree, although the specific field of study is not always relevant. They may also need to meet certain qualifications such as being ordained by their respective religious organization, completing theological training and being a member of the religious community they wish to serve.

The salary of a religious leader can vary widely depending on the type of religious organization they work for, their level of experience, and the size of the organization. According to the Bureau of Labor Statistics, the median annual salary for religious leaders is $48,930, with the top 10% earning more than $100,000. However, it's worth noting that the salary can vary greatly based on the type of religious organization they work for and the location and size of the market they work in. Additionally, some religious leaders may receive a smaller salary and may have other sources of income, such as a pension or income from other employment.

59. Social Media Manager

A social media manager is an individual who is responsible for managing an organization's presence on social media platforms such as Facebook, Twitter, and Instagram. They may work for a variety of organizations such as non-profits, government agencies, corporations, or as independent consultants. Social media managers can play an important role in the fight against human trafficking by raising awareness and educating the public about the issue through social media.

Social media managers can support anti-trafficking efforts by creating and managing social media campaigns to raise awareness about human trafficking. They can also use social media to provide information and resources to the public about the issue, such as the signs of trafficking, the impact it has on victims and society, and the steps that can be taken to combat it.

They can also collaborate with other organizations to share information and resources about human trafficking. Additionally, they can monitor and respond to online conversations about human trafficking, addressing misinformation and providing accurate information to the public.

To be an effective social media manager, it is important to have strong communication and interpersonal skills, be able to work well with a wide range of people, have knowledge of the issue of human trafficking, be able to effectively communicate the importance of addressing it, and have knowledge of social media platforms and the strategies and best practices for managing a social media presence. Strong analytical skills are also important for a social media manager to effectively measure the impact of their campaigns and make data-driven decisions.

A formal education is not always required to become a social media manager, but many successful social media managers have a degree in a related field such as marketing, communications, or journalism. However, on the job training and experience is also important for a social media manager.

The salary of a social media manager can vary widely depending on their level of experience, reputation, and the type of organization they work for. According to Glassdoor, the average salary for a social media manager is $52,994 per year, with the top 10% earning more than $89,000. However, it's worth noting that the salary can vary greatly based on the location and size of the market they work in, as well as the size and industry of the organization they work for.

60.Anthropologist

Anthropology is the study of human societies and cultures, including their origins, development, and behavior. Anthropologists often study the complex social, economic, and political factors that contribute to human trafficking and other forms of exploitation and violence. They can play an important role in the fight against human trafficking by providing valuable insights and perspectives on the cultural, social, and economic factors that contribute to human trafficking and by developing and implementing effective interventions and policies to address it.

Anthropologists can support anti-trafficking efforts by conducting research on the cultural, social, and economic factors that contribute to human trafficking. They can also study the experiences of victims and survivors of human trafficking to gain a deeper understanding of their needs and how to best support them. They can also develop and implement interventions and policies to address human trafficking and work with other professionals such as social workers and law enforcement to provide a comprehensive response to human trafficking.

To be an effective anthropologist, it is important to have strong analytical and critical thinking skills, be able to work well with a wide range of people, have knowledge of the issue of human trafficking, be able to effectively communicate the importance of addressing it, and have knowledge of the various methods and approaches used in anthropology. Strong oral and written communication skills are also essential for an anthropologist to effectively communicate research findings and recommendations to various stakeholders.

A formal education is required to become an anthropologist, typically a bachelor's or master's degree in anthropology. Some positions may require a PhD.

The salary of an anthropologist can vary widely depending on their level of experience, reputation, and the type of organization they work for. According to Glassdoor, the average salary for an anthropologist is $72,835 per year, with the top 10% earning more than $122,000. However, it's worth noting that the salary can vary greatly based on the location and size of the market they work in, as well as the size and industry of the organization they work for.

61. Economist

Economists study how societies, governments, businesses, households, and individuals allocate resources and make decisions. They can play an important role in the fight against human trafficking by providing valuable insights and perspectives on the economic factors that contribute to human trafficking and by developing and implementing effective interventions and policies to address it.

Economists can support anti-trafficking efforts by conducting research on the economic factors that contribute to human trafficking, such as poverty, unemployment, and lack of education and job opportunities. They can also study the impact of human trafficking on individuals, families, communities, and economies and analyze the effectiveness of different interventions and policies to address human trafficking. They can also work with other professionals such as social workers and law enforcement to provide a comprehensive response to human trafficking.

To be an effective economist, it is important to have strong analytical and critical thinking skills, be able to work well with a wide range of people, have knowledge of the issue of human trafficking, be able to effectively communicate the importance of addressing it, and have knowledge of economic theory, methods, and data analysis. Strong oral and written communication skills are also essential for an economist to effectively communicate research findings and recommendations to various stakeholders.

A formal education is required to become an economist, typically a bachelor's or master's degree in economics or a related field. Some positions may require a PhD.

The salary of an economist can vary widely depending on their level of experience, reputation, and the type of organization they work for. According to Glassdoor, the average salary for an economist is $93,632 per year, with the top 10% earning more than $155,000. However, it's worth noting that the salary can vary greatly based on the location and size of the market they work in, as well as the size and industry of the organization they work for.

62. Historian

Historians are responsible for studying and interpreting the past in order to understand and explain the present. They can play an important role in the fight against human trafficking by researching and documenting the history of human trafficking and providing context for the issue.

Historians can support anti-trafficking efforts by researching and documenting the history of human trafficking, which can provide valuable context for understanding the issue and how it has evolved over time. This can help to inform policy and programming decisions, as well as provide a deeper understanding of the root causes of human trafficking. Historians may also work with other professionals such as social workers and law enforcement to provide a comprehensive response to human trafficking.

To be an effective historian, it is important to have strong research and analytical skills, be able to work well with a wide range of people, have knowledge of the issue of human trafficking, be able to effectively communicate the importance of addressing it, and have knowledge of historical research methodologies and tools. Strong oral and written communication skills are also essential for a historian to effectively communicate information to the audience and other stakeholders.

A formal education is required to become a historian, typically a Master's degree or Ph.D in History. Many aspiring historians pursue a degree in history to gain the skills and knowledge needed for the job.

The salary of a Historian can vary widely depending on their level of experience, reputation, and the type of organization they work for. According to Glassdoor, the average salary for a Historian is $56,932 per year. However, it's worth noting that the salary can vary greatly based on the location and size of the market they work in, as well as the size and industry of the organization they work for.

63. Journalist

Journalists are responsible for researching, writing, and reporting on news and current events. They can play an important role in the fight against human trafficking by bringing attention to the issue and raising awareness among the general public.

Journalists can support anti-trafficking efforts by investigating and reporting on human trafficking cases, exposing the criminal networks involved, and shedding light on the experiences of survivors. Through their reporting, journalists can help to raise awareness of the issue among the general public, and put pressure on governments and organizations to take action. They can also collaborate with anti-trafficking organizations and other professionals such as social workers and law enforcement to provide a comprehensive response to human trafficking.

To be an effective journalist, it is important to have strong research and writing skills, be able to work well under pressure and tight deadlines, have knowledge of the issue of human trafficking, be able to effectively communicate the importance of addressing it, and have knowledge of the ethical principles of journalism. Strong oral and written communication skills are also essential for a journalist to effectively communicate information to the audience and other stakeholders.

A formal education is not always required to become a journalist, although a degree in journalism or a related field can be helpful. Many journalists begin their careers as interns or reporters at small newspapers or other media outlets.

The salary of a journalist can vary widely depending on their level of experience, reputation, and the type of organization they work for. According to Glassdoor, the average salary for a journalist is $48,856 per year. However, it's worth noting that the salary can vary greatly based on the location and size of the market they work in, as well as the size and industry of the organization they work for.

64. Government Relations Specialist

A government relations specialist is a professional who works to build and maintain relationships between an organization and government officials and agencies. This can include lobbying for laws and policies that support the organization's goals, as well as providing information and resources to government officials.

In the context of fighting human trafficking, a government relations specialist could work with organizations and coalitions to advocate for laws and policies that protect victims of human trafficking and hold traffickers accountable. They could also work with government agencies to ensure that they have the resources and training they need to effectively combat human trafficking.
Skills required to do well in this field include strong communication and negotiation skills, as well as knowledge of government processes and regulations. A background in political science, public policy, or law can be beneficial.

A college degree is typically required for a career as a government relations specialist, although a degree in a related field such as political science, public policy, or law can be beneficial. Some positions may also require a graduate degree.

Salaries for government relations specialists vary depending on the organization and location, but according to the Bureau of Labor Statistics, the median annual wage for this occupation is around $97,000.

65. Sociologist

A sociologist is a professional who studies the social behavior of individuals and groups in order to understand how society works and how social structures and institutions affect people's lives. They use a variety of research methods to collect and analyze data, and use this data to develop theories and explanations for social phenomena.

Sociologists can play an important role in the fight against human trafficking by studying the social and economic factors that contribute to the problem, and by identifying the most vulnerable populations. They can also use their expertise to design and evaluate interventions and programs aimed at preventing human trafficking and assisting victims. They can also work with other professionals, such as law enforcement and service providers, to develop a more comprehensive understanding of the issue.

To be an effective sociologist, one should have strong research skills, analytical skills, and the ability to think critically. A master's or Ph.D. degree in sociology is usually required for most research and academic positions, but some entry-level positions may only require a bachelor's degree.

Sociologists can make a median salary of $82,050 per year, according to the Bureau of Labor Statistics. However, the earning potential of sociologists can vary depending on their level of education and experience, as well as the type of employer and location.

In conclusion, being a sociologist can be an effective way to fight human trafficking by conducting research, identifying vulnerable populations and evaluating the effectiveness of interventions and programs. The skills and education required for this field are research, analytical skills, and critical thinking. The earning potential is also decent, with a median salary of $82,050 per year.

66. Artificial Intelligence Specialist:

Artificial Intelligence (AI) specialists are professionals who work with advanced computer systems and algorithms to develop intelligent machines and software that can process, analyze and make decisions on large amounts of data. They can be found in a wide range of fields and industries, including healthcare, finance, transportation, and manufacturing.

AI specialists can play an important role in the fight against human trafficking by developing and implementing technologies that can help identify and track traffickers and victims. They can also develop systems that can assist in investigations and prosecutions, as well as programs that can help identify and protect vulnerable populations. They can also work with other professionals, such as law enforcement and service providers, to develop a more comprehensive understanding of the issue.

To be an effective AI specialist, one should have strong programming skills, analytical skills, and a deep understanding of the field of AI. A bachelor's degree in computer science, mathematics, or a related field is usually required for most positions. Some employers may also require a master's degree or Ph.D. in a specialized field of study.

The earning potential for AI specialists is high, with a median salary of $146,085 per year according to Glassdoor. However, salaries can vary depending on the level of experience and education, as well as the type of employer and location.

In conclusion, being an AI specialist can be an effective way to fight human trafficking by developing and implementing technologies that can help identify and track traffickers and victims, and assist in investigations and prosecutions. The skills and education required for this field are strong programming skills, analytical skills, and a deep understanding of the field of AI. The earning potential for AI specialists is high, with a median salary of $146,085 per year.

67. Blockchain Specialist

Blockchain specialists are professionals who work with blockchain technology and cryptocurrencies. They are responsible for designing, developing, and maintaining the secure and decentralized networks that are the foundation of blockchain systems. They also work to create new applications and use cases for blockchain technology.

Blockchain specialists can play an important role in the fight against human trafficking by developing and implementing blockchain-based systems that can help identify and track traffickers and victims. They can also develop systems that can assist in investigations and prosecutions, as well as programs that can help identify and protect vulnerable populations. They can also work with other professionals, such as law enforcement and service providers, to develop a more comprehensive understanding of the issue.

To be an effective blockchain specialist, one should have strong programming skills, analytical skills, and a deep understanding of blockchain technology and cryptocurrencies. A bachelor's degree in computer science, mathematics, or a related field is usually required for most positions. Some employers may also require a master's degree or Ph.D. in a specialized field of study.

The earning potential for blockchain specialists is high, with a median salary of $130,000 per year according to Glassdoor. However, salaries can vary depending on the level of experience and education, as well as the type of employer and location.

68. Civil Affairs Officer

The Civil Affairs Officer is a critical role in the military that focuses on the civilian population and their relationship with the military. They are responsible for assessing the needs of the civilian population in areas where the military is operating, and working to build relationships with local leaders and organizations. Civil Affairs Officers also play a key role in coordinating with other organizations, such as non-governmental organizations and international organizations, to provide humanitarian assistance and support.

In the fight against human trafficking, Civil Affairs Officers can be used to assess the needs of vulnerable populations, such as refugees and internally displaced persons, who are at a high risk of being exploited by traffickers. They can also work with local leaders and organizations to build awareness of the issue and develop strategies to prevent trafficking in the area.

Additionally, Civil Affairs Officers can coordinate with other organizations, such as NGOs and international organizations, to provide support and assistance to victims of trafficking.

To be successful as a Civil Affairs Officer, individuals must possess strong communication and interpersonal skills, as well as the ability to think strategically and make sound decisions in a complex and ever-changing environment. They must also have a deep understanding of cultural differences and be able to navigate the political landscape in a given area. Additionally, Civil Affairs Officers must be able to work well in a team and be able to adapt to new and challenging situations.

The educational path to becoming a Civil Affairs Officer typically involves obtaining a bachelor's degree in a relevant field, such as international relations or political science. Some individuals may also pursue a master's degree in a related field. Additionally, Civil Affairs Officers must also complete Officer Candidate School and Civil Affairs Qualification Course.

According to the U.S. Bureau of Labor Statistics, the median annual salary for a military officer, including Civil Affairs Officers, is around $84,000. However, the salary can vary depending on a person's experience, rank, and location. Additionally, officers in the military may be eligible for other benefits, such as housing allowances, medical benefits, and retirement benefits.

69. Cyber Warfare Officer

The Cyber Warfare Officer is a specialized role in the military that focuses on the use of cyber technology for military operations. They are responsible for developing and implementing cyber strategies and tactics to protect military networks and systems, as well as conducting offensive operations to disrupt and degrade the capabilities of enemy forces. Cyber Warfare Officers also play a key role in coordinating with other organizations, such as government agencies and private sector partners, to share information and resources to defend against cyber threats.

In the fight against human trafficking, Cyber Warfare Officers can be used to disrupt the online networks and systems used by traffickers to recruit, transport, and exploit victims. This can include identifying and shutting down websites and social media accounts used by traffickers, as well as tracking and tracing online financial transactions used to fund trafficking operations. Additionally, Cyber Warfare Officers can work with other organizations, such as law enforcement agencies, to share information and resources to help identify and apprehend traffickers.

To be successful as a Cyber Warfare Officer, individuals must possess strong technical skills in areas such as computer science, network security, and programming. They must also have a deep understanding of cyber threats and be able to think strategically and make sound decisions in a fast-paced and ever-changing environment. Additionally, Cyber Warfare Officers must be able to work well in a team and be able to adapt to new and challenging situations.

The educational path to becoming a Cyber Warfare Officer typically involves obtaining a bachelor's degree in a relevant field, such as computer science, electrical engineering, or information technology. Some individuals may also pursue a master's degree in a related field. Additionally, Cyber Warfare Officers must also complete Officer Candidate School and Cyber Warfare Qualification Course.

According to the U.S. Bureau of Labor Statistics, the median annual salary for a military officer, including Cyber Warfare Officers, is around $84,000. However, the salary can vary depending on a person's experience, rank, and location. Additionally, officers in the military may be eligible for other benefits, such as housing allowances, medical benefits, and retirement benefits.

70. Legal Officer

A Legal Officer is a role within the military that provides legal advice and support to commanders and other military personnel. They are responsible for interpreting and applying laws, regulations, and policies that govern military operations and activities. Legal Officers also play a key role in advising commanders on legal issues related to the use of force and the treatment of prisoners of war. They also provide legal support for military justice matters and claims.

In the fight against human trafficking, Legal Officers can be used to advise commanders on the legal aspects of trafficking operations and the prosecution of traffickers. They can also provide legal support to law enforcement agencies and other organizations in the investigation and prosecution of trafficking cases. Additionally, Legal Officers can work with other organizations, such as NGOs and international organizations, to advise on international legal frameworks related to human trafficking.

To be successful as a Legal Officer, individuals must possess strong legal skills and a deep understanding of the laws and regulations that govern military operations and activities. They must also have excellent analytical and critical thinking skills and be able to think strategically and make sound decisions in a complex and ever-changing environment. Additionally, Legal Officers must be able to work well in a team and be able to adapt to new and challenging situations.

The educational path to becoming a Legal Officer typically involves obtaining a bachelor's degree and then going to law school to obtain a law degree (JD). After that, legal officers must also complete Officer Candidate School and Legal Officer Basic Course. According to the U.S. Bureau of Labor Statistics, the median annual salary for a military officer, including Legal Officers, is around

$84,000. However, the salary can vary depending on a person's experience, rank, and location. Additionally, officers in the military may be eligible for other benefits, such as housing allowances, medical benefits, and retirement benefits.

71. Logistics Officer

A Logistics Officer is a role within the military that is responsible for planning and managing the movement, supply, and maintenance of military equipment, personnel, and resources. They are responsible for ensuring that troops in the field have the supplies and support they need to carry out their mission. Logistics Officers also play a key role in coordinating with other organizations, such as government agencies and private sector partners, to share information and resources to support military operations.

In the fight against human trafficking, Logistics Officers can be used to plan and manage the movement of personnel and resources to support anti-trafficking operations. This can include identifying and securing transportation and accommodation for law enforcement personnel and victims of trafficking, as well as managing the supply of equipment and other resources needed to support operations. Additionally, Logistics Officers can work with other organizations, such as NGOs and international organizations, to share information and resources to support anti-trafficking operations.

To be successful as a Logistics Officer, individuals must possess strong organizational and planning skills, as well as the ability to think strategically and make sound decisions in a fast-paced and ever-changing environment. They must also have a deep understanding of logistics and supply chain management and be able to work well in a team and adapt to new and challenging situations.

The educational path to becoming a Logistics Officer typically involves obtaining a bachelor's degree in a relevant field, such as logistics, supply chain management, or business administration. Some individuals may also pursue a master's degree in a related field. Additionally, Logistics Officers must also complete Officer Candidate School and Logistics Officer Basic Course.

According to the U.S. Bureau of Labor Statistics, the median annual salary for a military officer, including Logistics Officers, is around $84,000. However, the salary can vary depending on a person's experience, rank, and location. Additionally, officers in the military may be eligible for other benefits, such as housing allowances, medical benefits, and retirement benefits.

72. Military Intelligence Officer

Military Intelligence Officer is a role within the military that is responsible for collecting, analyzing, and disseminating intelligence information that supports military operations. They are responsible for providing commanders with information on the enemy, the battlefield, and other factors that may impact military operations. Military Intelligence Officers also play a key role in coordinating with other organizations, such as government agencies and private sector partners, to share information and resources to support military operations.

In the fight against human trafficking, Military Intelligence Officers can be used to collect and analyze information on trafficking networks and patterns. This can include identifying key individuals and organizations involved in trafficking, as well as tracking the movement of victims and traffickers. Additionally, Military Intelligence Officers can work with other organizations, such as law enforcement agencies, to share information and resources to support anti-trafficking operations.

To be successful as a Military Intelligence Officer, individuals must possess strong analytical and critical thinking skills, as well as the ability to think strategically and make sound decisions in a complex and ever-changing environment. They must also have a deep understanding of intelligence gathering and analysis, and be able to work well in a team and adapt to new and challenging situations.

The educational path to becoming a Military Intelligence Officer typically involves obtaining a bachelor's degree in a relevant field, such as international relations, political science, or a related field. Additionally, Military Intelligence Officers must also complete

Officer Candidate School and Military Intelligence Officer Basic Course.

According to the U.S. Bureau of Labor Statistics, the median annual salary for a military officer, including Military Intelligence Officers, is around $84,000. However, the salary can vary depending on a person's experience, rank, and location. Additionally, officers in the military may be eligible for other benefits, such as housing allowances, medical benefits, and retirement benefits.

73. Cybercrime Investigator

A Cybercrime investigator is a professional who is responsible for investigating and solving cybercrime cases. They use their technical and forensic skills to collect and analyze digital evidence, identify suspects, and build cases against them. They may work for law enforcement agencies, private companies, or government organizations.

In the fight against human trafficking, Cybercrime investigators can play an important role by identifying and disrupting the digital networks used by traffickers to recruit, transport, and exploit victims. They can also track and trace online financial transactions used to fund trafficking operations. Additionally, Cybercrime investigators can work with other organizations, such as NGOs and international organizations, to provide support and assistance to victims of trafficking.

To be successful as a Cybercrime investigator, individuals must possess strong technical skills in areas such as computer science, network security, and forensic analysis. They must also have a deep understanding of cybercrime and be able to think strategically and make sound decisions in a fast-paced and ever-changing environment. Additionally, Cybercrime investigators must be able to work well in a team and be able to adapt to new and challenging situations.

The educational path to becoming a Cybercrime investigator typically involves obtaining a bachelor's degree in a relevant field, such as computer science, electrical engineering, or forensic science.

Some individuals may also pursue a master's degree in a related field. Additionally, Cybercrime investigators may also complete specific training and certifications related to cybercrime investigations.

The salary for a Cybercrime investigator can vary depending on factors such as the employer, location, and experience. According to PayScale, the median salary for a Cybercrime investigator is around $75,000 per year.

74. Digital Forensics Analyst

A Digital Forensics Analyst is a professional who is responsible for identifying, preserving, analyzing, and presenting digital evidence. They use specialized techniques and tools to recover data from various digital devices and platforms, such as computers, mobile phones, and servers. They may work for law enforcement agencies, private companies, or government organizations.

In the fight against human trafficking, Digital Forensics Analysts can play an important role by recovering digital evidence that can be used to identify and prosecute traffickers. They can also provide support to victims of trafficking by recovering evidence of their exploitation. Additionally, Digital Forensics Analysts can work with other organizations, such as NGOs and international organizations, to provide support and assistance to victims of trafficking.

To be successful as a Digital Forensics Analyst, individuals must possess strong technical skills in areas such as computer science, network security, and forensic analysis. They must also have a deep understanding of digital forensics and be able to think strategically and make sound decisions in a fast-paced and ever-changing environment. Additionally, Digital Forensics Analysts must be able to work well in a team and be able to adapt to new and challenging situations.

The educational path to becoming a Digital Forensics Analyst typically involves obtaining a bachelor's degree in a relevant field, such as computer science, electrical engineering, or forensic science. Some individuals may also pursue a master's degree in a related field. Additionally, Digital Forensics Analysts may also complete specific training and certifications related to digital forensics.

The salary for a Digital Forensics Analyst can vary depending on factors such as the employer, location, and experience. According to the PayScale, the median salary for a Digital Forensics Analyst is around $70,000 per year.

75. Intelligence Analyst

An Intelligence Analyst is a professional who is responsible for collecting, analyzing, and disseminating intelligence information. They use various methods, such as open-source intelligence, human intelligence, and signals intelligence, to gather information and provide insights on issues of national security, such as terrorism, espionage, and cyber threats. They may work for law enforcement agencies, private companies, or government organizations.

In the fight against human trafficking, Intelligence Analysts can play an important role by collecting and analyzing information on trafficking networks and patterns. This can include identifying key individuals and organizations involved in trafficking, as well as tracking the movement of victims and traffickers. Additionally, Intelligence Analysts can work with other organizations, such as law enforcement agencies, to share information and resources to support anti-trafficking operations.

To be successful as an Intelligence Analyst, individuals must possess strong analytical and critical thinking skills, as well as the ability to think strategically and make sound decisions in a complex and ever-changing environment. They must also have a deep understanding of intelligence gathering and analysis, and be able to work well in a team and adapt to new and challenging situations.

The educational path to becoming an Intelligence Analyst typically involves obtaining a bachelor's degree in a relevant field, such as international relations, political science, or a related field. Additionally, Intelligence Analysts may also complete specific training and certifications related to intelligence analysis.

The salary for an Intelligence Analyst can vary depending on factors such as the employer, location, and experience. According to the PayScale, the median salary for an Intelligence Analyst is around $71,000 per year.

76.Open Source Intelligence Analyst

Open-source Intelligence (OSINT) Analyst is a professional who is responsible for collecting and analyzing publicly available information to support decision making and strategic planning. They use various methods, such as online research, social media monitoring, and data mining, to gather information from publicly available sources, such as news articles, social media posts, and government publications. They may work for law enforcement agencies, private companies, or government organizations.

In the fight against human trafficking, OSINT Analysts can play an important role by collecting and analyzing publicly available information on trafficking networks and patterns. This can include identifying key individuals and organizations involved in trafficking, as well as tracking the movement of victims and traffickers. Additionally, OSINT Analysts can work with other organizations, such as law enforcement agencies, to share information and resources to support anti-trafficking operations.

To be successful as an OSINT Analyst, individuals must possess strong research and analytical skills, as well as the ability to think strategically and make sound decisions in a fast-paced and ever-changing environment. They must also have a deep understanding of open-source intelligence and be able to work well in a team and adapt to new and challenging situations.

The educational path to becoming an OSINT Analyst typically involves obtaining a bachelor's degree in a relevant field, such as international relations, political science, or a related field. Additionally, OSINT Analysts may also complete specific training and certifications related to open-source intelligence analysis.

The salary for a Open-Source Intelligence (OSINT) Analyst can vary depending on factors such as the employer, location, and experience.

According to Payscale, the median salary for an Open-source Intelligence Analyst is around $70,000 per year. However, it can range from $50,000 to $90,000 per year. Note that this can also vary depending on the industry that the OSINT Analyst works in, as well as the specific skills and experience they bring to the role.

77. Social Media Intelligence Analyst

A Social Media Intelligence (SOCMINT) Analyst is a professional who is responsible for collecting and analyzing information from social media platforms to support decision making and strategic planning. They use various methods, such as online research, social media monitoring, and data mining, to gather information from social media platforms, such as Facebook, Twitter, and Instagram. They may work for law enforcement agencies, private companies, or government organizations.

In the fight against human trafficking, SOCMINT Analysts can play an important role by collecting and analyzing information from social media platforms on trafficking networks and patterns. This can include identifying key individuals and organizations involved in trafficking, as well as tracking the movement of victims and traffickers. Additionally, SOCMINT Analysts can work with other organizations, such as law enforcement agencies, to share information and resources to support anti-trafficking operations.

To be successful as a SOCMINT Analyst, individuals must possess strong research and analytical skills, as well as the ability to think strategically and make sound decisions in a fast-paced and ever-changing environment. They must also have a deep understanding of social media platforms and be able to work well in a team and adapt to new and challenging situations.

The educational path to becoming a SOCMINT Analyst typically involves obtaining a bachelor's degree in a relevant field, such as computer science, electrical engineering, or a related field. Additionally, SOCMINT Analysts may also complete specific training and certifications related to social media intelligence analysis.

The salary for a Social Media Intelligence (SOCMINT) Analyst can vary depending on factors such as the employer, location, and experience. According to Payscale, the median salary for a Social Media Intelligence Analyst is around $70,000 per year. However, it can range from $50,000 to $90,000 per year. Note that this can also vary depending on the industry that the SOCMINT Analyst works in, as well as the specific skills and experience they bring to the role.

78. Threat Intelligence Analyst

A Threat Intelligence Analyst is a professional who is responsible for identifying and analyzing potential threats to an organization, such as cyber attacks, fraud, and espionage. They use various methods, such as open-source intelligence, network traffic analysis, and incident response, to gather information on potential threats and provide insights on how to mitigate them. They may work for law enforcement agencies, private companies, or government organizations.

In the fight against human trafficking, Threat Intelligence Analysts can play an important role by identifying and analyzing potential threats to anti-trafficking operations. This can include identifying and tracking the activities of criminal organizations involved in trafficking, as well as identifying and mitigating the risks of cyber attacks on anti-trafficking systems and infrastructure. Additionally, Threat Intelligence Analysts can work with other organizations, such as law enforcement agencies, to share information and resources to support anti-trafficking operations.

To be successful as a Threat Intelligence Analyst, individuals must possess strong analytical and critical thinking skills, as well as the ability to think strategically and make sound decisions in a fast-paced and ever-changing environment. They must also have a deep understanding of cyber security and be able to work well in a team and adapt to new and challenging situations.

The educational path to becoming a Threat Intelligence Analyst typically involves obtaining a bachelor's degree in a relevant field, such as computer science, electrical engineering, or a related field.

Additionally, Threat Intelligence Analysts may also complete specific training and certifications related to threat intelligence analysis.

The salary for a Threat Intelligence Analyst can vary depending on factors such as the employer, location, and experience. According to Payscale, the median salary for a Threat Intelligence Analyst is around $85,000 per year. However, it can range from $60,000 to $120,000 per year. Note that this can also vary depending on the industry that the Threat Intelligence Analyst works in, as well as the specific skills and experience they bring to the role.

79. Web Intelligence Analyst

A Web Intelligence Analyst is a professional who is responsible for collecting and analyzing information from the web to support decision making and strategic planning. They use various methods, such as online research, web scraping, and data mining, to gather information from various sources on the internet, such as websites, forums, and social media platforms. They may work for law enforcement agencies, private companies, or government organizations.

In the fight against human trafficking, Web Intelligence Analysts can play an important role by collecting and analyzing information from the web on trafficking networks and patterns. This can include identifying key individuals and organizations involved in trafficking, as well as tracking the movement of victims and traffickers. Additionally, Web Intelligence Analysts can work with other organizations, such as law enforcement agencies, to share information and resources to support anti-trafficking operations.

To be successful as a Web Intelligence Analyst, individuals must possess strong research and analytical skills, as well as the ability to think strategically and make sound decisions in a fast-paced and ever-changing environment. They must also have a deep understanding of the internet and be able to work well in a team and adapt to new and challenging situations.

The educational path to becoming a Web Intelligence Analyst typically involves obtaining a bachelor's degree in a relevant field, such as computer science, electrical engineering, or a related field. Additionally, Web Intelligence Analysts may also complete specific training and certifications related to web intelligence analysis.

The salary for a Web Intelligence Analyst can vary depending on factors such as the employer, location, and experience. According to Payscale, the median salary for a Web Intelligence Analyst is around $70,000 per year. However, it can range from $50,000 to $90,000 per year. Note that this can also vary depending on the industry that the Web Intelligence Analyst works in, as well as the specific skills and experience they bring to the role.

Printed in Great Britain
by Amazon